D1521426

HIDDEN
CHICAGO
LANDMARKS

HIDDEN
CHICAGO
LANDMARKS

JOHN R. SCHMIDT

THE
History
PRESS

Published by The History Press
Charleston, SC
www.historypress.com

First published 2019

ISBN 9781540239662

Library of Congress Control Number: 2019936987

CONTENTS

CONTENTS

CONTENTS

ACKNOWLEDGEMENTS

Most of my research was carried out at the Regenstein Library of the University of Chicago, as well as at the Harold Washington Library in downtown Chicago. My thanks to the staffs at both places. And big thank-yous to Ben Gibson and Ryan Finn at The History Press for steering this book through to publication.

My wife, Terri Schmidt, has been her usual wise, witty and patient self during my work. I have already dedicated four books to her, because she deserves it. But this time, the dedication will be to my two other favorite people in the world: my adult children, Nick Schmidt and Tracy Samantha Schmidt.

A.M.D.G.

INTRODUCTION

When I was thirty years old, I bought my first house. I had already been teaching history for several years and was well along working on my doctorate. Yet I didn't learn until months later that I was living down the block from a historic house of singular notoriety. That started me collecting the material that eventually wound up in this book.

Hidden Chicago Landmarks is a descriptive guide to the places that aren't included on the typical tour. Here are those neglected historic sites. Here also are some historic sites that should have been preserved but were not. And here is the Chicagoland version of "flyover country"—some notable neighborhoods that most people simply drive by on their way to somewhere else.

The name "Chicagoland" was popularized by the *Chicago Tribune* to describe the area it serviced. Besides the city itself, the suburbs and exurbs were included. That is the territory covered here. Leave the political boundaries to the politicians.

Locations of historic sites have been identified through contemporary newspaper articles, city directories and census records. Secondary sources have been checked against these primary sources. It should be noted that Chicago's address numbers were revised in the early twentieth century. I have listed all sites with their modern addresses. My source for converting the old address numbers is the book *Plan of Re-Numbering, City of Chicago*, first published in 1909 and now available online.

Introduction

Here are a few things to note as you dive into the book. Chicago is generally a safe place. Still, like any large city, parts of it can be dangerous. If you are unsure about visiting a particular site, check out the crime statistics. Also, remember that many of the historic homes described here are still private residences. Unless a property operates as a museum, respect the people who live there. Don't bother them.

Shorter versions of some stories have appeared on my blog. And if you are still wondering what historic house got me started on this adventure, don't worry. That house is here in the book.

Part I

HIDDEN LANDMARKS

CENTRAL AND WEST

The Cowpath in the Loop

There's a service door next to the main entrance of the Hyatt Centric Hotel at 100 West Monroe Street. Step through it and you enter a quaint bit of Chicago history. Chicago was incorporated as a town in 1833. That same year, a man named Willard Jones purchased a ninety-foot-wide parcel of land northwest of Clark and Monroe Streets from the State of Illinois. The price was $200.

Not much is known about Willard Jones. Some sources tell us he was a farmer. Whatever his occupation, he could appreciate rising land values. In 1844 Jones sold the southern half of his property to Royal Barnes. However, Barnes got only an eighty-foot-wide lot, with Jones retaining title to a ten-foot-wide strip at the west end. There was pasture land to the south, where the Board of Trade now stands. Presumably, Jones kept that corridor along the western edge so he could lead his cows out to graze.

Two years after the Barnes sale, Jones sold the northern half of his original property to Abner Henderson. Written into the deed was a provision that Henderson would have access to Monroe Street via that ten-foot corridor west of the Barnes land.

Decades passed. Chicago burned and was rebuilt. Now linked on its north end to an alley off Madison Street, the Willard Jones cowpath became part of a block-long passageway behind the buildings on Clark Street. It looked like an ordinary alley.

Then, in 1926, the owners of the old Barnes property hired architect Frank Chase to design a twenty-two-story office building at Monroe and Clark. By then they had acquired title to the ten-foot access corridor on the western edge of their plot. But the owners of the Henderson land to the north still had that right-of-way guarantee and refused to surrender it.

Perhaps the Henderson group was looking for a payoff to relinquish their claims. If so, they were disappointed. Architect Chase redrew his plans. In the end, the 100 West Monroe Building was constructed with an eighteen-foot-high tunnel through its western edge, big enough for any farm animals or hay wagons that might be passing through the Loop. The revised construction, coupled with the loss of rental property, reportedly cost $350,000.

A cowpath in the middle of the skyscrapers—it was a wonderfully quirky bit of local color. In a 1937 ceremony, Mayor Edward J. Kelly affixed a bronze historic marker on the side of the building. The text read, "Historic Cowpath: This areaway 10 x 177 x 18 feet is reserved forever as a cowpath by terms of the deed of Willard Jones in 1844, when he sold portions of the surrounding property. Erected by Chicago's Charter Jubilee and Authenticated by the Chicago Historical Society."

The city's official recognition sealed the matter. The tale of Willard Jones and his deed was retold in the *WPA Guide to Illinois* and other reference volumes. Much to the owners' chagrin, the 100 West Monroe Building

Monroe Street access to the Loop cowpath, the small doorway to the left of the Hyatt Centric Hotel main entrance. *Photo by the author.*

came to be known as the "cowpath building." A 1946 report that noted the passageway had never been a dedicated street didn't seem to change its status. However, doors were now installed at each end of the path, to discourage neighbors from using it as a garbage dump. Sometime during the 1950s, Mayor Kelly's plaque disappeared.

In 1969 the First National Bank of Chicago built an annex north of the 100 West Monroe Building. The new annex blocked off the northern part of the cowpath, diverting traffic into an east–west alley. According to a 1979 *Chicago Tribune* article, both Chicago Title & Trust and the Chicago Historical Society declared that the action was legal. There don't seem to have been any court challenges to it.

When Hyatt began converting the 100 West Monroe Building into a hotel in 2012, connoisseurs of Chicago trivia feared that the cowpath would be totally obliterated. Happily, the hotel management has a sense of history and has preserved it. You can still use the bovine tunnel as a shortcut through to LaSalle Street, if that is your pleasure. And Hyatt has also shown a sense of whimsy. One of the hotel's conference rooms is named for Willard Jones.

DILLINGER WANNABE

Almost any guidebook of Chicago historic sites will include the Biograph Theater on Lincoln Avenue, where the feds finally nailed bank robber John Dillinger in 1934. It's a favorite stop for gangster tours too.

A few miles away, at 2040 West Potomac Avenue, there is a forgotten landmark of similar pedigree. In 1955 the city's greatest manhunt since Dillinger ended at this nondescript two-flat. This is where Chicago police captured Richard Carpenter.

Born in 1929 and raised in Chicago, Carpenter had a long record of trouble, including a dishonorable discharge from the army and a 1951 arrest for accidentally shooting his mother. He drifted through a series of jobs. Convicted in a holdup, he served time and then escaped.

By the summer of 1955, Carpenter had been a fugitive for eighteen months. Chicago police considered him a prime suspect in a series of nearly one hundred robberies on the North and West Sides. It was all small-time stuff—saloons, grocery stores, isolated pedestrians and so on.

On August 16 Detective William Murphy recognized Carpenter on a subway train and arrested him. At the Roosevelt Road station, a block from police headquarters, Murphy became distracted for a moment while reaching for an identification poster in his pocket. Carpenter pulled out a gun and shot the detective dead. Running up the subway stairs to the street, he commandeered a car at gunpoint and escaped.

Chicago police launched a massive dragnet. One of their own had been killed. They searched all of Carpenter's known haunts, but with no success. He had disappeared into the anonymous city.

The next evening, Patrolman Clarence Kerr was using his off-duty hours to take in a movie with his wife at the Biltmore Theater on Division Street. As they were leaving, he spotted a man sleeping in the rear row. The man looked like Carpenter. Kerr sent his wife into the lobby and then shook the sleeping man.

It was Carpenter. Kerr put him under arrest and Carpenter complied. On the way up the aisle, Carpenter pretended to stumble. In a flash he had his gun out. Shots rang through the empty theater. Officer Kerr fell to the floor, wounded in the chest. Carpenter escaped out the emergency exit.

Carpenter had been hit in the leg in the exchange of gunfire. Looking for a hideout, he limped over to Potomac Avenue. He began breaking through the rear screen door of the two-flat at no. 2040. The truck driver who lived there heard the noise and went to investigate. He found a sweating, bleeding Carpenter pointing a pistol at him.

"I'm Carpenter," he told the truck driver. "I just shot another policeman. If you behave you won't get hurt. If not, I'll shoot you. Now let me in!" The truck driver's wife and two small children were also at home. Carpenter joined them, settled in and began pondering what he would do next.

Meanwhile, the citywide search went on. It was the early days of television, and the new medium breathlessly reported on the hunt for "Cop-Killer Carpenter." Some parents used the widely publicized fugitive as a bogeyman to threaten reluctant children—"I don't care if you want to stay out ten minutes longer. Get inside now, or Carpenter will get you!"

By the evening of August 18, Carpenter had been holed up on Potomac Avenue nearly twenty-four hours. He dropped his guard. He let the truck driver's wife take the children out for some fresh air. Then he allowed the truck driver to step out.

The truck driver immediately alerted the police. The building was surrounded. Searchlights filled the sky, a helicopter hovered overhead. Two thousand people gathered on the street. The bullhorn blared, "Carpenter! Come out with your hands up!"

Carpenter tried to get away, jumping into the open window of an apartment next door. Again there was gunfire. But this time, the police got

The two-flat on Potomac Avenue where "Cop-Killer Carpenter" was captured. *Photo by the author.*

their man. And if Carpenter thought he'd become a bad-boy folk hero like Dillinger, he was mistaken. As the cops led him away, the crowd on Potomac Avenue shouted, "Kill him! Kill him!"

Richard Carpenter was convicted of murder and died in the electric chair in 1958. His onetime hideout on Potomac Avenue is privately owned.

WALT DISNEY BIRTHPLACE

The cottage at 2156 North Tripp Avenue was unremarkable. Until recently, even the neighbors knew nothing about its historic significance. This is the house where Walt Disney was born.

Elias Disney and Flora Call, Walt's parents, married in Florida in 1888. Elias operated an orange grove with little success and then took a job delivering mail. By 1890 the Disneys had one son, and another baby was on the way. That spring, they moved to Chicago.

A world's fair coming in 1893. Construction was booming all over the city. Elias had no trouble finding work as a carpenter. The family first rented a cottage on the South Side, a few miles from the fair site.

Elias's brother had preceded him to Chicago and had opened a small hotel. Elias also wanted to get back into business. With the money he was earning from his carpentry work, he purchased a plot of land in the Hermosa district on the city's Northwest Side in the fall of 1891. The area was sparsely populated, with dirt streets and few buildings.

The Disneys' property was located on the southwest corner of Tripp Avenue and Palmer Street. Over the course of eighteen months, Elias worked on putting up a house in his spare time. The finished product was a two-story frame cottage. The family settled in during the first months of 1893.

Elias did well in Hermosa. He went into business with another carpenter, bought more lots, built more cottages and sold them. Sometimes Flora was able to come out and help the men on the construction jobs. The partners kept one of the cottages as a rental unit.

The Disneys were also becoming active in the local Congregational church. Elias became a trustee and served on the building committee. Sometimes he'd give the Sunday sermon if the minister had been called away. "He was a pretty good preacher," his wife said.

Walter Elias Disney was the family's fourth son. He was born in the second-floor bedroom of the Tripp Avenue cottage on December 5, 1901. The story that he was named after the church pastor is probably not true. The story that he was adopted, and actually born in Spain, is definitely not true. Like many people born in 1901, Walt Disney did not have an official birth certificate, and that led to the later confusion.

Walt Disney's birthplace, before its restoration as a museum. *Photo by the author.*

The Disneys stayed on Tripp Avenue until 1906. That winter, two boys from church families tried to pull off a robbery and wound up killing a policeman. Elias decided he didn't want to raise his sons in the city. He sold his house for $1,800, unloaded his half of the rental cottage down the block and moved his family to a remote farm in central Missouri.

Walt had just turned four. He'd later have no memories of the Tripp Avenue house. But in 1917, after living in various places and trying different occupations, Elias Disney moved the family back to Chicago. He had invested in a jelly-making factory.

The new Disney home was on the Near West Side, at 1523 West Ogden Avenue. Walt enrolled as a freshman at McKinley High School. He drew cartoons for the school paper and took art classes at night but left after one year to become an ambulance driver in World War I. He never again lived in Chicago.

Both Elias and Flora Disney lived long enough to see their youngest son become a Hollywood studio magnate. Walt Disney himself died in 1966. And no—his body is not frozen in some cryogenic warehouse.

As mentioned, the Disney birthplace was long an undiscovered landmark. The original address was 1249 Tripp Avenue. Although Chicago street numbers were revised in 1909, many sources continued to list the house with the old number, sending unwitting tourists a few miles south to Tripp and 13th Street.

That confusion should be at an end. In 2013 the cottage was purchased by a California couple who announced plans to restore it as a museum and community resource. The Walt Disney Company later pledged $250,000 to help advance the project. At this writing, the work goes on.

HEF'S GALEWOOD HOMESTEAD

Many Chicago tours will take time to point out the massive, elegant brick-and-limestone building at 1340 North State Street. Today, it is divided into condos. In an earlier era, it was the original Playboy Mansion. Hugh Hefner lived here from 1959 through 1975 before decamping to Los Angeles. This is where he perfected the persona and lifestyle that made him famous—or notorious, depending on your point of view.

The South Side apartment building where Hefner created *Playboy* magazine is long gone. But his childhood home has survived on the city's far West Side, at 1922 North New England Avenue.

Hugh Hefner was four years old when his family moved into the newly built brick home in the Galewood section of Austin. His father, Glenn, was an accountant, and his mother, Grace, was a homemaker and part-time teacher. The year was 1930, and the Depression was just getting underway. Glenn had to work long hours to scrape by, leaving the raising of Hugh and his younger brother mostly to his wife.

The Galewood neighborhood was still sparsely settled during the 1930s. Hugh remembered growing up amid prairies and prairie animals, with gas streetlamps and milk delivered from horse-drawn wagons. During the week, he went to the Sayre Elementary School, a few blocks from his home. Sundays meant services at the local Methodist church.

Hugh was an underachiever at Sayre. Teachers observed that he was intelligent yet would work hard only at things that interested him. He seemed to be living in a world of his own. He liked to write stories and was especially skilled as a cartoonist.

At Steinmetz High School, Hugh reinvented himself. Outside the circle of his closest friends, he'd always been shy. Now he upgraded his wardrobe, adopted a confident demeanor and literally forced himself to become more outgoing. He also began referring to himself in the third person as "Hef." "I became the imaginary adolescent, the teenager I wanted to be," he later said.

It paid off. By sophomore year, Hefner had become the leader of the school's self-styled sophisticates. He wrote copy and drew cartoons for the school newspaper, appeared in plays and even produced his own fifteen-minute horror film. As a senior, he was elected president of the student council.

Hefner graduated from Steinmetz in January 1944. World War II was on, and shortly afterward he enlisted in the army. Trained as an infantry rifleman, he wound up serving stateside as a clerk. He was discharged as a corporal in 1946.

Hefner used the G.I. Bill to attend the University of Illinois–Urbana. His girlfriend, Millie Williams, was already a student there. He graduated from the accelerated program with a degree in psychology in 1949, married Millie and returned to Chicago.

The newlyweds moved in with Glenn and Grace on New England Avenue. They made do with a single large bedroom. Postwar housing was in short supply, and they didn't have much money anyway. While Millie worked at the nearby Mars candy factory, Hugh drifted through a series of jobs. He enrolled in a graduate program in sociology at Northwestern but dropped out after one semester.

The house in Galewood where little Hugh Hefner dreamed of becoming a playboy. *Photo by the author.*

In the spring of 1952, Millie Hefner became pregnant. The couple finally moved out of the house in Galewood, renting an apartment at 6052 South Harper Avenue. Hugh saw his cosmopolitan new neighborhood near the University of Chicago as "a sort of Greenwich Village." It was here that he put together his magazine in the fall of 1953.

Hugh's parents continued to live on New England Avenue while their elder son became famous. Glenn Hefner died in 1976. Grace sold the house and moved to Arizona nine years later. She died in 1997, at the age of 102.

Hugh Hefner made a number of sentimental journeys back to Galewood in the years following his move to Los Angeles. The 1992 documentary *Hugh Hefner: Once Upon a Time* includes scenes from one such trip. After his death in 2017, there was discussion about turning his boyhood home into a museum. Nothing has been done yet, and the house remains a private residence.

CARL SANDBURG'S FIRST HOUSE

Hog Butcher for the World,
Tool Maker, Stacker of Wheat,
Player with Railroads and the Nation's Freight Handler;
Stormy, husky, brawling,
City of the Big Shoulders…

There was a time when every child in a Chicago school learned those words. They are the opening lines of Carl Sandburg's poem "Chicago."

Sandburg was born in Galesburg in 1878, the son of Swedish immigrants. As a young man he drifted through a series of jobs—milkman, bricklayer, fireman, soldier, hobo, political organizer for the Social Democratic Party. Then he got married.

Sandburg and his wife, Lillian, settled in Chicago in 1912. Carl became a reporter at a small newspaper and rented an apartment at 4646 North Hermitage Avenue in Uptown. While living there he wrote "Chicago." It was published in the March 1914 issue of *Poetry* magazine.

Soon after the poem appeared, Sandburg abandoned the city in favor of a suburb. He bought a small frame house at 616 South 8th Avenue in Maywood. The purchase was facilitated by a $500 loan from a family friend.

The couple was thrilled to have a place of their own, where they could "start growing things in our own soil." There was already a cherry tree in the backyard suitable for producing pies and preserves. They added beds of strawberries and gooseberries and started a vegetable garden. Carl converted a second-floor bedroom overlooking the cherry tree into his study.

He'd been writing stories and poetry for years, with little success. Now that began to change. Sandburg's collection *Chicago Poems* appeared in 1916. Then he landed a reporter's job at a "real newspaper," the *Chicago Daily News*. In 1919, now with three young daughters to raise, he moved to a larger house at 331 South York Street in Elmhurst.

There were more poetry anthologies, a book on the 1919 Chicago race riot and a series of children's books. Sandburg was gaining a national reputation. His publisher suggested he write a Lincoln biography for young people. In 1926 he emerged from his research with *Abraham Lincoln: The Prairie Years*. The children's book had morphed into an adult book in two volumes.

The Lincoln book was a bestseller and ended Sandburg's financial worries. The book also made him a literary lion. For the rest of his long life, he was as famous for being Carl Sandburg as for anything he wrote.

Sandburg moved from Elmhurst to Michigan in 1930 and eventually settled in the hill country of North Carolina. The Lincoln biography grew to a total of six volumes with the publication of *Abraham Lincoln: The War Years*. He won three Pulitzer prizes, two for poetry and one for the Lincoln books. He even won a Grammy for his narration of Aaron Copland's *Lincoln Portrait*.

Although he lived elsewhere after 1930, Sandburg remained one of Chicago's favorite sons. In 1960 his name was used on an urban renewal project, Sandburg Village, designed to provide affordable rental units while stabilizing the west end of the Gold Coast. And he often returned to the city that made him famous. When suburban Orland Park named a high school in his honor, Sandburg came to the dedication and had a grand time, telling stories and singing ballads.

He had been a workingman. He always cultivated the image of the people's poet, with rumpled clothing and unkempt hair. A few years after the dedication, he decided to revisit "his" high school. By then, a different principal was in charge. The new man thought Sandburg was a panhandler and threw him out.

Carl Sandburg died in 1967. Some years earlier, he had summed up his philosophy this way: "What I need mainly is three things in life, possibly four—to be out of jail, to eat regular, to get what I write printed, and then a little love at home and a little outside."

Sandburg's first house still stands on 8th Avenue in Maywood, a private residence. The Hermitage Avenue home in the city is recognized with an official "Chicago Tribute" marker and is also a private residence. The house in Elmhurst was torn down many years ago.

SAM GIANCANA HOME

Oak Park has three historic districts and dozens of historic buildings. There is no official recognition of the bungalow on the northwest corner of Wenonah and Fillmore Avenues. This is where mob boss Sam Giancana lived—and where he was murdered.

He was born in the Taylor Street Italian settlement in 1908. Depending on the source you consult, his birth name was Momo Giancana or Salvatore Giangana or Gilormo Giancana. As a teenager he demonstrated his particular talents by putting together a gang of neighborhood toughs. He caught the attention of recruiters for the Capone team, and in 1925, at seventeen, Giancana moved up to the big leagues.

His first job with Capone was as a driver of fast cars, still a rare and sought-after skill in 1925. After serving that apprenticeship, Giancana became an all-purpose gunman. He was arrested a number of times but never convicted. In 1933 he married and moved into a three-flat at 2822 West Lexington Street.

Giancana continued climbing the gangland organizational ladder using methods that can best be left to the imagination. He served a short prison sentence for operating an illegal still. During World War II he was rejected for military service. The reason given was a "constitutional psychopathic state and inadequate personality, manifested in strong anti-social tendencies."

By now Giancana had three daughters. In 1945 he purchased the bungalow at 1147 South Wenonah Avenue in Oak Park for $32,000. That's about $450,000 in today's money—and he paid cash.

The family joined St. Bernardine Parish in nearby Forest Park. Although Sam wasn't often seen at Mass, his daughter Antoinette remembered that he donated an altar rail to the church. That particular gift has since been removed.

Giancana lived quietly in Oak Park. He didn't bother his neighbors, and they certainly didn't bother him. He was devoted to his wife, Angeline, but that didn't stop him from becoming involved with other women. Mrs. Giancana died in 1954, and Sam never remarried.

As the 1950s moved into the 1960s, Giancana became the public face of the Chicago Outfit. He was always in the news. In the 1960 election, Giancana and his minions allegedly stole enough Illinois votes to swing the state—and the presidency—to John F. Kennedy. So when the Kennedy administration began cracking down on organized crime, Giancana felt double-crossed. This scenario claims that Kennedy's assassination was actually a mob hit.

Giancana was also rumored to be part of a CIA plot to kill Cuban leader Fidel Castro. After complications arose, the new plan was to embarrass

The landmark Oak Park tries to forget—Sam Giancana's home. *Photo by the author.*

Castro by slipping him a drug that would cause his beard to fall off. Whatever the truth, Castro kept power—and his beard.

Then there were Giancana's lady friends. He was linked to a number of high-profile movie stars. One of his mistresses, Judith Campbell Exner, was also involved with President Kennedy. Dark hints circulated that Exner had acted as a liaison between the mob and the White House.

In 1965 Giancana was jailed for refusing to testify before a grand jury but soon released. Organized crime likes to operate under the radar whenever possible. Giancana was simply getting too much publicity. He was forced out as head of the Chicago Outfit. He retired to a villa in Mexico but kept the Oak Park house.

The feds brought Giancana back to the United States for further questioning late in 1974. He was scheduled to appear before a Senate subcommittee. Before he could testify, he was killed in his basement. The date was June 19, 1975. He had been frying some sausage on a stove when he was shot in the back. He'd apparently trusted the person who murdered him. The case remains unsolved.

A few years after Giancana's death, I bought a house down the block on Wenonah Avenue. I remembered the killing, but it was not until moving in that I realized I'd be living near such a notable site. The only thing my neighbors said about Sam Giancana was that they missed the FBI men who used to keep his place under surveillance. Having them around 24/7 made the neighborhood feel safer.

CONTINENTAL DIVIDE

Most of Chicago is as flat as a pancake. As a result, even the slightest bump in the landscape is magnified out of proportion by local boosters. We have communities within the city named Calumet Heights and Mount Greenwood and Washington Heights and Archer Heights. The few rises that gave these places such names would be laughed at in San Francisco.

But size alone doesn't make significance. A case in point is the ridge that runs along the general line of Narragansett Avenue, through the Northwest Side and into Oak Park.

Long ago Lake Michigan was much larger, and its waters covered most of what is now the city of Chicago. The Narragansett ridge marked one of the ancient lake's beach lines. At 630 feet above sea level, it is about 50 feet higher than the lake's current level.

Chicago was settled because of its convenient location between two great water systems. Think of the native peoples—or Marquette and Jolliet—paddling their canoes down Lake Michigan and the Chicago River, portaging a few miles over the ridge and then catching the Des Plaines River on the way to the Mississippi. The opening of the Illinois-Michigan Canal in 1848 eliminated the portage with the first direct water link between the two rivers. Then came an even greater project.

Early settlers used the Chicago River as a garbage dump. The river's natural course empties into Lake Michigan, so all the waste of civilization began to mingle with the city's drinking water. You will sometimes read that 10 percent, 20 percent or even 30 percent of Chicago's population died in a cholera epidemic in those years. The figures are wildly exaggerated. But there was a public health problem.

The solution was to reverse the flow of the Chicago River. A new, larger waterway—the Chicago Drainage Canal—was dug through the ridge to connect the two water systems. A barrier was built to close off the Chicago River from Lake Michigan. In 1900 the canal locks were opened, and the river began flowing backward, as it has done ever since.

The Chicago Drainage Canal was celebrated as the greatest engineering feat since the pyramids. Every local guidebook told tourists about the only river in the world that flowed backward. The story was repeated so often and grew so old that most people began to tune it out. Then, in 1999, the Village of Oak Park began erecting signs along its portion of the ridge. The signs identified the ridge as a "continental divide."

The reason for the designation is simple. Rain that falls on the east of the ridge eventually flows into the Atlantic Ocean. Rain that falls on the west of the ridge goes toward the Mississippi River and the Gulf of Mexico. A retired architect named Bill Dring had located an old map that identified the ridge as the St. Lawrence Divide, because the east-flowing waters from the ridge reach the Atlantic via the St. Lawrence River. Impressed with Dring's research, Oak Park officials put up the signs.

A few spoilsports have claimed that Oak Park's ridge is not an actual continental divide. Drop a bottle into the water and send it west from the ridge toward the Mississippi and the Gulf. If the bottle doesn't get picked up or smashed, after all its adventures that bottle is still going to be carried through the Gulf and wind up in the Atlantic Ocean anyway. So what's the big deal?

That's a pretty technical argument. If you want to get even more technical, consider that more than 70 percent of the earth's surface is

Chicagoland's own continental divide, where you can straddle two great river systems. *Photo by the author.*

water, and all of that water flows together at some place or another. Using that line of reasoning, the continents are really nothing more than giant islands. That means you have to throw out the Rocky Mountain Divide too. Now you're getting silly.

Most of us will never get to Four Corners and never be able to stand in four states at once. But with very little effort, we can straddle two great watersheds. So let's all celebrate Oak Park's own continental divide. And while we are at it, let's put up a few more signs to recognize it.

THE PALACE ON 12TH STREET

Before television or videogames or the Internet, everyone went to the movies—all the time. Movie theaters became opulent palaces. In Chicago, it all began on the West Side in the North Lawndale neighborhood.

The Balabans were a Russian Jewish family. In 1907 one of the teenage sons got a job singing in a tiny vaudeville theater on Kedzie Avenue. The place also featured the fifteen-minute movie shorts of the time. One day the boy's mother came to the theater.

Mrs. Balaban was impressed by the business model. "People pay on the way in—nobody can owe us money!" she said. And rather than having live performances, showing films had an advantage. Movies could be rented cheaply, without a large cash outlay for actors, sets and musicians. Everything came prepackaged. So the Balabans rounded up $400 and rented a theater. They had their own nickelodeon. (Since admission was five cents, the first movie theaters came to be called nickleodeons.) Like the little place on Kedzie, the Balabans had a storefront operation, with a few folding chairs and a bedsheet for a screen. Such primitive accommodations were acceptable in 1907.

But that was already changing. Movies were becoming more and more popular. Filmmakers responded by producing more elaborate cinema. The process was crowned in 1915 with the three-hour epic *The Birth of a Nation*.

The Balabans witnessed this evolution. Reasoning that grander films deserved grander theaters, they adapted to the changing times. In the fall of 1917, just ten years after they'd leased that first nickelodeon, they opened the Central Park Theatre at 3535 West 12th Street (now Roosevelt Road).

The Central Park was arguably the world's first movie palace. Designed by the firm of Rapp & Rapp, the 1,780-seat theater was a versatile venue that could be used for either films or live performances. A large center stage was flanked by two smaller stages decorated with plants and statues. Colored stage lighting took in the whole house. Between the main floor and the balcony, at the mezzanine level, were a series of boxes that stretched around the auditorium perimeter in a horseshoe arrangement. They made the audience feel like they were part of the stage set.

As a bonus, the Central Park was air-conditioned. Theaters normally closed during July and August then. A few struggled to stay open by having fans blow over strategically placed blocks of ice. But one of the Balabans had worked in the meatpacking business, where refrigeration to cool large rooms had been developed. That process was adopted in their new building. During the dog days of summer, people flocked to the Central Park just to cool off. The doors opened at 9:30 a.m. most mornings and didn't close until midnight. If you had a dime and you had the time, you could take a mini-vacation on 12th Street.

By now the family business was known as Balaban & Katz. When the Central Park proved a success, they built other movie palaces. Eventually B&K operated thirty-six theaters in the city and suburbs, including such Loop landmarks as the Chicago, the Oriental, the Roosevelt and the United Artists.

America's first movie palace, the Central Park Theatre, as it looks today. *Photo by the author.*

The Central Park also rates a footnote in the history of American music. In 1921 Benny Goodman made his professional debut playing the clarinet on one of the theater's Jazz Nights. The future "King of Swing" was then twelve years old.

During the 1960s, as TV became more popular, many movie theaters closed. The Central Park was converted into a church in 1971. In 2004 the theater once more scheduled a movie. The onetime Jewish neighborhood of North Lawndale had become African American, and the film was *Within Our Gates*, produced by a black filmmaker in 1920 as a response to the racism of *The Birth of a Nation*.

In recognition of its pioneer status, the Central Park Theatre has been placed in the National Register of Historic Places. More recently, the century-old building has been showing its age. In 2013 news stories reported that city inspectors had found extensive code violations, with an estimated repair price of $300,000. At this writing, the future of Chicago's pioneer movie palace is uncertain.

ANTON J. CERMAK HOME

In our time, the South Lawndale neighborhood is the heart of Chicago's Mexican community. A century ago, the people there were mostly Czech.

The splendid brick residence at 2348 South Millard Avenue dates from that era. This was the home of Mayor Anton J. Cermak.

Cermak was a master politician. He is usually credited with putting together the Chicago Democratic Machine, an identification that has passed into popular culture. On Kelsey Grammer's TV series *Boss*, his fictional Chicago mayor, Tom Kaine, often talked wistfully about his real-life predecessor. People want to be led, Kaine says. And although he "utterly lacked charisma," Cermak was a leader.

Cermak was born in what was then known as Bohemia in 1873. Soon afterward, his family moved to America. Anton grew up in the coal town of Braidwood, Illinois. He had about two years of formal education, going down into the mines at twelve. A few years later, when the mines began to play out, the Cermaks moved once more, to Chicago.

They settled among the other Czechs in South Lawndale. As Anton advanced through his teens and into young manhood, he developed skill with his fists and a high capacity for alcoholic beverages. He became leader of a local "saloon gang." He started the first of many businesses, selling kindling wood from a horse-drawn cart.

He also went into Democratic politics. Over the course of thirty years, Cermak worked his way from the ground up—assistant precinct captain, precinct captain, ward committeeman, state representative, alderman, municipal court bailiff and alderman again. His businesses prospered. He became rich. And as Prohibition descended on the land, Cermak became head of the United Societies for Local Self-Government, a lobbying group of great influence—an NRA for booze rather than for guns.

Cermak was elected president of the Cook County Board of Commissioners in 1922. He had become a political force to be reckoned with. He wanted to be mayor of Chicago, but he hadn't yet consolidated his power. He did have the clout to get the new county courthouse and jail located in South Lawndale, on California Avenue at 26th Street.

His Millard Avenue home was built in 1920. The architects were Frank Randak and James B. Rezny, who designed several other buildings in the neighborhood. As it happened, Cermak wound up living in the house less than ten years. After his wife died in 1928, he moved into a suite at the Congress Hotel downtown, to be closer to his work.

By 1931 Cermak was chairman of the Cook County Democratic Party and finally ready to run for mayor. The Depression was getting worse, and the city growing tired of Big Bill Thompson. Cermak won easily. Although he resigned his chairmanship when he assumed the mayor's chair, Cermak remained the unquestioned boss of the party.

He campaigned loyally for Franklin D. Roosevelt in the 1932 presidential election. Still, he had been late getting on the bandwagon, and when Roosevelt won, Cermak needed to mend political fences. That's what Chicago's mayor was doing in Miami Beach on February 15, 1933, a few weeks before inauguration day.

Roosevelt was at a waterfront park, speaking to a crowd from the back seat of an open car. After his speech, he noticed Cermak and called him over.

Token from Anton Cermak's 1922 campaign for president of the Cook County Board—and yes, casting two votes was legal in this election. *Author's collection.*

The two men were chatting when a deranged anarchist pulled out a gun and began shooting. Roosevelt was unharmed, but Cermak was hit. As he was bundled into Roosevelt's car to be driven to the hospital, he supposedly told the president-elect, "The country needs you. I'm glad it was me and not you." Three weeks later, Anton Cermak was dead.

That's right. When it was all over, and despite his looming presence in the history of Chicago politics, Cermak didn't get a chance to do much as mayor. Michael Bilandic had more time in the office than he did.

So great were the crowds wanting to pay respects to the martyred mayor that Cermak's funeral was held in the Chicago Stadium and broadcast over radio. An estimated 150,000 people were on hand to witness his entombment at Bohemian National Cemetery. A few days later, the city council renamed 22nd Street as Cermak Road. Today, the Millard Avenue home is a private residence.

ST. PAUL CATHOLIC CHURCH

With its twin spires soaring over the surrounding cottages, St. Paul Catholic Church is visually stunning, calling to mind the medieval cathedrals of Western Europe. And the story of St. Paul's construction does follow that model.

The parish was established in 1876. Many Catholic parishes were then organized on an ethnic basis, and St. Paul was founded to serve Germans living south and west of 18th and Halsted Streets. The Great Fire of 1871 had destroyed a large part of the North Side German settlement. With the new McCormick Reaper Works opening at Western and Blue Island Avenues, the Lower West Side attracted many displaced German families.

St. Paul's first services were held in private homes. As more people joined the congregation, an unused stable was moved to the southwest corner of Hoyne Avenue and 22nd Place to serve as a temporary church, and a four-room school was built. The foundations for a permanent church were laid on the property in 1886. Then Father George Heldmann became pastor.

Heldmann had a grand vision for St. Paul parish and inspired his people to share in it. To make homeownership affordable for the local immigrant families, parishioners organized the St. Paul Savings and Loan Association, which would eventually become one of the five largest S&Ls in the state. The little school building was expanded. Heldmann also took a deeper look at the plans for the new church. He wasn't satisfied with them.

In 1897 Heldmann had the old foundation filled in and hired the young architect Henry Schlacks to build a grander structure. Schlacks came up with a twin-tower Gothic design. He felt it would remind the parishioners of the churches they'd left behind in the old country, most notably the famous Cologne Cathedral.

Schlacks himself became the general contractor. The parishioners included many skilled masons and bricklayers, who did much of the labor in their spare time. The materials used, as well as the traditional construction methods, earned St. Paul the nickname "the church built without a nail." The exterior walls were completed in only two years, allowing the church to be formally dedicated in the summer of 1899. The signature front towers were finished the following year.

Work on the main altar and other parts of the interior went on in stages over the next three decades. Even as he became a celebrated designer of churches, Henry Schlacks counted St. Paul as a favorite project. He often returned to tweak his creation. Like any work of art, the church was a living thing.

Father George Heldmann had built well but not wisely. In rushing to finish the church and complete his other projects, he had plunged the parish into serious debt. In 1903 the archbishop removed him as pastor.

Still, the people did have their church. St. Paul was the first brick Gothic church in America, reputed to be fireproof. At 245 feet tall, the twin towers

St. Paul Catholic Church, a Gothic marvel on the Lower West Side. *Photo by the author.*

were higher than most Loop office buildings. The main pulpit was fashioned from Carrara marble. The Venetian mosaics and the stained-glass windows were worthy of the finest old-world cathedral.

As the years passed, the German families who founded the parish dispersed to other parts of the city, and their place was taken by Poles and Czechs. In the 1960s, Mexicans began moving into the Lower West Side. Today, they form the greater part of St. Paul's congregation.

To the untrained eye, the church building itself seemed to be aging gracefully—it even served as the backdrop to a memorable nighttime sequence in the 1987 movie *The Untouchables*. However, an engineering report in 2008 noted serious structural problems. A major overhaul was needed.

Chicago was already losing such treasures as St. John of God Church and Temple Anshe Kanesses Israel, and there were fears that St. Paul was also doomed. The parishioners launched a restoration effort, contributing as much of their personal labor as modern liability laws would allow. The archdiocese added a timely allocation of $10 million. The church was saved.

Although it's off the beaten path from most city tours, St. Paul Church is worth a visit. Just head out west from the Loop and look for the spires.

Marquette Monolith

Jacques Marquette (1637–1675) was a French Jesuit missionary. After working in what is now northern Michigan, he joined the explorer Louis Jolliet on an expedition along the upper Mississippi River in 1673. During their travels, the party learned about a portage between the Des Plaines River and Lake Michigan. They used the shortcut on their way back home.

Marquette had made friends and converts among the native peoples. In 1674 he embarked on a journey to visit the Illiniwek tribes. He spent the winter of 1674–75 in a cabin somewhere along that convenient portage between the river and the lake before returning to Michigan. There Marquette fell ill and died, not quite thirty-eight years old.

Because of his winter sojourn on the portage, Marquette is often credited as being the first non-indigenous resident of Chicago. A heroic statue of the priest stands at the south end of Marshall Boulevard, where it bends into 24th Street. Trailing just behind him are the figures of Jolliet and an anonymous native friend. The memorial was dedicated in 1926.

The Jacques Marquette monument is prominently sited along a heavily traveled auto route. Less well known is our current subject, the Marquette Monolith. Located near the south branch of the Chicago River, at 2635 South Damen Avenue, the monolith is supposed to mark the site where Marquette spent his historic winter. Trouble is, nobody knows for sure where Marquette made his camp.

Some scholars have suggested other locations, such as Olympia Fields or Palos Hills. The Damen Avenue site was determined by an amateur historian named Ossian Guthrie, based on comparisons between Marquette's journals and local topography. In 1905 Guthrie presented his research to the Chicago Historical Society. He then led a group of society members on a field trip to the area, and they endorsed his findings.

Guthrie's Marquette cabin site soon received official recognition from the City of Chicago. Neighborhood leaders were thrilled. A local lumber company erected a fifteen-foot-tall mahogany cross with a bronze plaque on the spot in 1906, with the French consul in attendance at the dedication. The cross became a point of pride for the city's newly assimilated Catholic population.

Chicago winters aren't kind to mahogany. By the 1920s, the cross was deteriorating. Besides that, the city planned on building a bigger bridge over the river, and the cross was in the way. A new, sturdier, relocated monument seemed to be the best solution.

Monolith marking the site where Father Jacques Marquette may have wintered. *Photo by the author.*

So, in 1930, the cross was replaced with a fifteen-foot-tall granite monolith, headed with the single word "MARQUETTE." The main feature of the Deco slab is a bronze bas-relief of the priest greeting an Indian. At the bottom, a plaque explains the significance of the monument.

The plaque itself is a window into the times the monolith was built. The dedication date is rendered as "Anno Domini MCMXXX," as if the Roman numerals had the magic power to make the slab last as long as the Colosseum or the Arch of Constantine. Yet the name of the good father is Anglicized as "James Marquette." If you are going to translate "Jacques" into the local idiom, why bother with Roman numerals on the same plaque?

The text goes on to tell us about Marquette's historic importance, of how his journals touted the region's soil, climate and transportation facilities. Although we can appreciate the advantages of soil and transportation facilities, it's doubtful that Chicago's climate is a selling point.

One thing about the plaque always catches the viewer's eye: the swastikas. The hooked cross was an ancient symbol of good luck that Hitler appropriated. Until the Nazis made them notorious, you'd see swastikas in many innocent places. Be assured that there is nothing sinister about their placement here. However, in light of the controversies swirling around old monuments in recent years, perhaps we will hear demands that the swastikas be covered over with more innocuous symbols.

The Marquette Monolith is located in the middle of an industrial area and gets little tourist traffic. Still, the city has honored the missionary-explorer in a more notable way. Jacques Marquette is one of the few people to have two official, full-fledged Chicago streets named after him: Marquette Road at 6700 South and Marquette Avenue at 2700 East.

CLARENCE WAGNER'S BRIDGE

In 2014 the Chicago Circle Interchange of three expressways was renamed the Jane Byrne Interchange, in honor of a onetime Chicago mayor. The new name has quickly entered common usage. Yet few motorists who continue driving east on the Eisenhower realize that the bridge carrying them over the Chicago River is officially named for Clarence Wagner.

At one time, Wagner was one of Chicago's most powerful politicians— perhaps *the* most powerful. In 1953 he was Fourteenth Ward alderman, chairman of the council's Finance Committee and Democratic ward committeeman. Mayor Martin Kennelly was well meaning but weak, so Wagner practically ran the city.

Clarence Wagner was born in Chicago in 1904. Although he carried his German father's surname, he was always quick to point out that his mother's heritage was Irish. That ethnic identity was most advantageous in South Side Democratic politics. Young Clarence caught the eye of the local ward boss and moved up steadily in the organization.

He was elected alderman in 1942. But more importantly, Wagner became the ward committeeman in 1947, giving him a place at the center of power where he could build alliances and gather influence. "He was a bright and audacious lawyer with a sardonic sense of humor," one reporter remembered. Because of his distinctive voice, friends called him "Gravels."

In July 1953, Cook County Democratic committeemen held a meeting to choose a new chairman. It was assumed the post would go to County Clerk Richard J. Daley. Party insiders whispered that Daley would then challenge Kennelly for mayor in the 1955 primary. But at the meeting, Alderman Wagner asked that the vote for chairman be delayed two weeks. His motion carried. The meeting adjourned, with Daley still just another committeeman. You can read different explanations of what Wagner was up to. Most likely, he'd decided he was just as qualified as Daley to be county chairman—or mayor.

In the meantime, Wagner took a short fishing vacation with another politician and their young sons. The alderman was at the wheel of his

Clarence Wagner Memorial Bridge, a forgotten tribute to a forgotten political kingpin. *Photo by the author.*

Cadillac on a Minnesota road the morning of July 10 when he missed a turn and crashed the car. Although the passengers escaped with injuries, Clarence Wagner was killed.

Mayor Kennelly wept when he heard the news. So did many other politicos, for Alderman Wagner was well liked. Crowds packed the wake at his home on May Street and the funeral Mass at Visitation Church. One hundred cops were put on special duty to keep the traffic moving.

Would Wagner have become mayor if he'd lived? We will never know. Daley did become party chairman and did oust Kennelly from the mayor's chair in 1955. And, of course, Daley the Younger later won the office.

But the Daleys weren't the only political dynasty that arose with Clarence Wagner's death. The man chosen to succeed Wagner as Fourteenth Ward committeeman and alderman was Joseph Burke, who held both posts until he died in 1968. Joseph Burke was then followed by his son, Edward Burke, who eventually became the longest-serving alderman in Chicago history.

A few days after Wagner's death, the Chicago City Council met to consider a way to honor its fallen member. The Congress Expressway was then under construction on the West Side. Someone proposed that the new double bridge over the Chicago River be designated the Clarence Wagner Memorial Bridge, and the council adopted the idea. No one seemed to grasp the irony of naming an expressway bridge after someone who'd been killed in an auto accident.

The official name of the bridge never entered the vernacular. Guidebooks didn't cite it, and there are conflicting reports on whether the bridge ever sported a "Clarence Wagner" plaque. Certainly two generations of Mayors Daley never pushed to give an old rival more visible recognition.

In 2012 the bridge underwent extensive rehabilitation. I retold Clarence Wagner's story on my blog then, suggesting that it might be an appropriate time to put up a plaque. Finally, on July 10, 2013—the sixtieth anniversary of the alderman's death—the city rededicated Clarence Wagner's bridge. Alderman Edward Burke had spearheaded the effort and spoke at the ceremony. For anyone who is interested, the new plaque is on the southeast bridge house.

THE BALBO COLUMN

In 1933 Chicago staged a world's fair in Burnham Park. July 15 marked one of the fair's highlights. Shortly after 6:00 p.m., the Balbo Air Squadron arrived in the waters of Lake Michigan.

Aviation was still exciting and dangerous in 1933—only six years had passed since Lindbergh's transatlantic flight. Now General Italo Balbo, head of the Italian air force, had brought his fleet of twenty-four seaplanes on a goodwill trip from Rome to Chicago. Because of bad weather and an accident along the way, the journey had taken two weeks.

But now they were here, safely moored off Navy Pier. A few minutes after the landing, Balbo himself strolled onto the deck of his seaplane, coolly surveying the cheering thousands who had gathered on shore—he looked as if he were "going to afternoon tea," one reporter wrote. He lit a cigarette and smiled.

For the next three days, the city went Balbo-crazy. The general and his fliers were feted with a rally in Soldier Field, speeches, parades, banquets and official proclamations. Seventh Street was renamed Balbo Drive. The hoopla was later spoofed by the Marx Brothers in their movie *A Night at the Opera*. Then, at the end of the three days, the intrepid crew flew back to Rome.

That's the way it looked in 1933. But as Paul Harvey used to say, now for the rest of the story.

The Italian government that sponsored the Balbo Air Squadron was the fascist government of Benito Mussolini. Balbo himself was a true believer, often referred to as the Duce's "right-hand man." The brutality of the fascist regime was already well known. Yet many apologists accepted such difficulties as the price of progress. One bit of wisdom declared, "Mussolini may be bad, but he makes the trains run on time."

Chicago's most controversial public monument, the Balbo Column. *Photo by the author.*

Mussolini also knew something about public relations. On the first anniversary of the flight, he sent Chicago an ancient temple column as a gift—although he sent it by ship, and not by plane. Balbo himself spoke from Rome via radio-phone at the dedication ceremony. "Let this column stand as a symbol of increasing friendship between the people of Italy and the people of the United States," the general said. The Balbo Column, as it became known, was erected in the park east of Soldier Field.

General Italo Balbo was killed in 1940 when his plane was hit by friendly fire. There was suspicion that Mussolini ordered an assassination to remove a popular rival.

Following fascist Italy's defeat in World War II, the new government's ambassador to the United States suggested that marks of respect to the Mussolini regime be removed. Shortly afterward, a Chicago alderman proposed renaming Balbo Drive, although nothing was said about the Balbo Column. In any case, both the street name and the column remained.

Time appeared to heal the wounds of war. In 1973 the Museum of Science and Industry celebrated the fortieth anniversary of the Balbo Air Squadron with a special exhibit. Each year, there were fewer and fewer irate letters demanding that the street name be changed or the monument be removed. Most Chicagoans figured that the street was named Vasco Núñez Balboa, after the Spanish explorer who sighted the Pacific Ocean.

There was no mistaking what the Balbo Column was about. Carved into its base was a florid inscription in Italian declaring that "Fascist Italy Under the Auspices of Benito Mussolini" was presenting this monument to the city of Chicago in honor of the Balbo Squadron. Instead of 1933, the date of the historic flight is given as "The Eleventh Year of the Fascist Era."

In 2017 the protests over Confederate statues and other dated artifacts caused Chicagoans to revisit the Balbo question. Once again, there were calls to change the name of Balbo Drive.

What to do with the Balbo Column is not so easily resolved—after all, its pedigree predates the "Fascist Era" by two millennia. The area where it stands is now known as Gold Star Families Memorial Park, in honor of police officers who have been killed in the line of duty. Why not put a new plaque on the column and rededicate it to them?

WHO IS BURIED IN LOGAN'S TOMB?

General John Logan
Sits on a horse
On top of a hill
In Grant Park in Chicago.

That once-popular nursery rhyme describes a statue. Pictures of the general-on-the-horse-on-the-hill were flashed around the world in 1968, when the Democratic National Convention was in town, and protesters found it a convenient rallying point. But who was General John Logan? And more to the point of our story, what is that hill doing there?

John Alexander Logan was a Civil War general and a two-term U.S. senator from Illinois. He was the driving force behind establishing Memorial Day as a national holiday. In 1884 Logan became the running mate of Republican presidential nominee James G. Blaine. Although the Blaine-Logan ticket lost by a whisker, Logan was established as one of the front-runners for the next presidential election. Then, in December 1886, the general suddenly died.

Logan was given the rare honor of lying in state in the U.S. Capitol rotunda. He was buried at Rock Creek Cemetery in the District of Columbia. Meanwhile, back in Logan's native state, a plan was taking shape.

Former president Ulysses S. Grant—*the* great Civil War general—had died in 1885. Grant had been a citizen of Illinois, but New York City was building a mausoleum to house his remains. Now Chicago had an opportunity to one-up those eastern body-snatchers. Chicago would build an even grander mausoleum for General Logan.

Three days after Logan's death, the Chicago City Council voted to donate land for his tomb. The South Park Commissioners and the Illinois state legislature soon got on the bandwagon. A total of $64,000 was appropriated for the project—serious money in 1886.

Mary Logan, the general's widow, preferred to have her husband buried in the District. However, she agreed to give way to the Chicago plan. When Mrs. Logan visited the city the following summer, newspaper reports said she was arranging the transfer of the general's remains.

The general's body was moved on the second anniversary of his death, December 26, 1888. But he didn't go to Chicago. Instead, he was simply transported across Washington and interred at the National Soldiers Home Cemetery. Grave robbing was a concern in those times—thieves had nearly made off with Lincoln's body—and Mrs. Logan felt that security was better at the general's latest home.

Meanwhile, work on the Chicago tomb moved forward. In 1891 Augustus Saint-Gaudens was given the commission of creating an equestrian statue for the proposed mausoleum. There was some discussion about putting the tomb in Jackson Park in time for the upcoming Columbian Exposition. However, both the commissioners and the general's widow decided that the location was too remote. A site in Lakefront (Grant) Park east of 9th Street was finally chosen.

John Logan's statue (and prospective tomb) in Grant Park. *Photo by the author.*

Saint-Gaudens's statue of Logan was dedicated in 1897. The heroic sculpture captured a famous incident in the general's military career, when Logan grabbed the battle flag from a fallen comrade and rallied his troops at the Battle of Atlanta. It was a remarkably lifelike piece of art, the *Chicago Tribune* declared, with "the snorting of the responsive steed [seeming] to echo in your ears as you look upon the statue." The large mound on which it stood could easily be converted to a tomb.

Mrs. Logan attended the dedication ceremony and was visibly touched. But by now she'd changed her mind about bringing her husband with her to Chicago. Mary Logan had carved out a career for herself as a journalist, lecturer and world traveler. She was comfortable on the East Coast.

Still, she kept an interest in her husband's Chicago monument. When the park commissioners concluded that there would be no Logan Tomb off 9th Street, they decided to move the statue and re-landscape the site. Mary Logan was not pleased. She noted pointedly that Saint-Gaudens was recognized as America's greatest sculptor, the siting in the park was perfect and "it would be outrageous to interfere with it."

So, the general stayed in Washington, and his aborted tomb stayed in Grant Park. As for Chicago, it has had to make do honoring John Logan with that Logan statue, Logan Square, Logan Boulevard, Logan Elementary School and the Logan Square Community Area.

Part II

HIDDEN LANDMARKS

NORTH

Fairbank Row Houses

A group of limestone row houses has stood at 1234–52 North State Street since 1890. Designed by architect Charles Palmer, they were originally rental units. The buildings are collectively known as the Fairbank Row Houses after the longtime residents of no. 1244, Mr. and Mrs. Kellogg Fairbank.

Kellogg Fairbank was an honest, upright, somewhat dull lawyer who spent much of his time managing the estate of his late father, Chicago's lard and soap king. He is part of our story only as an introduction to his wife.

Janet Ayer Fairbank was also a Chicago blueblood. Yet while raising three children and performing all the duties expected of a society matron of her era, she found time to do more. She wrote magazine articles and novels and promoted women's suffrage. She also became active in party politics, serving on the Democratic National Committee from 1924 to 1928. It was from her townhouse that Mrs. Fairbank helped launch the political career of Adlai Stevenson. The issue was garbage.

Stevenson came from a political family. When he was born in 1900, his grandfather, the first Adlai Stevenson, had already been vice president of the United States. The younger Adlai was also attracted to public service. He became acquainted with the Fairbanks during the 1920s while he was working as a corporate lawyer. By 1935 Stevenson and his growing family were living in the townhouse next door to them, at no. 1246.

That January, garbage collection on the 1200 block of North State Street had been slow. This being Chicago and Mrs. Fairbank having some clout, she simply phoned her good friend Mayor Edward J. Kelly. The garbage was promptly picked up.

Mrs. Fairbank was aware that her young neighbor was interested in a political career. She offered Stevenson some advice. "I think we have made history by having the mayor intervene personally about garbage collection," she told Adlai. "I think it would please the mayor if you wrote him on your office stationery, so that he realizes that you are a valuable Democratic friend."

So, Stevenson took pen in hand. He did write to Mayor Kelly, and he laid it on thick. "Your prompt and effective response was very gratifying," he wrote. "To a good Democrat, it is cumulative evidence of the fine service your administration is rendering in even the smallest details."

Stevenson's letter produced the desired effect. Within a few days, the mayor responded with a cordial note. From that time on, young Adlai had his foot in the door at city hall. He began making friends among the party regulars. Later in the year, Stevenson moved off State Street to a farm in Libertyville. He was called to Washington for several assignments during the next dozen years. But he kept in contact with the boys back in Chicago.

It paid off in 1948. The Democrats needed a strong candidate for governor of Illinois. They wanted a person of sterling reputation who was

The Fairbank Row Houses, where a Gold Coast society woman nudged Adlai Stevenson into politics. *Photo by the author.*

also a loyal member of the party. Stevenson was the obvious choice; he was slated and elected. In 1952 and 1956 he was the Democratic Party's candidate for president of the United States. Although he lost both times, Stevenson made enough of an impression on Chicago politics to have the Southwest Expressway renamed in his honor after he died in 1965.

Meanwhile, Mrs. Fairbank remained busy. Each New Year's Day until her death in 1951, she hosted a gala all-day reception that attracted society folk, writers, opera singers, social activists and cigar-chewing politicians. At most places it would have been an unlikely gathering. Here it was just a reflection of the many interests of the hostess.

There is a companion story of Gold Coast garbage that should be mentioned. It seems that a wealthy Astor Street chatelaine ran into Mayor Kelly at a social gathering and complained about the trash pickup on her street. Kelly phoned Paddy Bauler, the saloonkeeper-alderman whose ward included part of the Gold Coast.

"How many votes did you get in that lady's precinct in the last election?" Bauler asked Kelly. The mayor said he didn't know.

"I didn't get any," Bauler said. "Let the lady pick up her own garbage!"

CIDER HOUSE STORY

Chicago history is more than just a fire. But sooner or later, there's bound to be a story of the Great Conflagration of 1871. The house at 2121 North Hudson Avenue is at the center of this particular tale.

The Chicago Fire started on the Near South Side on Sunday evening, October 8. Pushed on by strong southwest winds, it burned through downtown, jumped the river and continued moving north. Nothing in its path seemed safe.

By the second evening the fire had advanced more than three miles, passing Center Street (today's Armitage Avenue). Here the buildings were fewer and farther apart. On Hudson Avenue, the only house was a little wooden cottage belonging to a policeman named Richard Bellinger.

Bellinger had built the house for his new bride two years earlier. It was their dream come true. As he looked to the south, Bellinger could see the wall of flames coming closer and closer. He could feel the air getting hotter. Hell was bearing down on him, but he would not surrender. He would save their home.

The sidewalks were wooden and would feed the flames. Bellinger tore them up. He tore up his picket fence and front stairs. He grabbed buckets and bottles and cups and whatever else was handy, filling them with water from the cistern. Then he sat down to wait.

He did not wait long. Sparks from the onrushing fire started to hit the front porch, and Bellinger quickly doused them. The fire kept coming, Bellinger kept pouring water. He ran around the four sides of the little cottage. He climbed onto the roof. He dropped back to the ground. Wherever the flames lit, Bellinger was there to put them out.

He grew tired. He lost track of time. But he was winning. The flames around him were almost gone. And then—he ran out of water! Was all his hard toil for nothing? All he needed was a bucket or two more! Oh, cruel twist of fate!

But wait! Bellinger remembered the barrel of apple cider in the cellar. He told his wife to draw some of the cider into the buckets. And with this last little bit of liquid, the valiant policeman was able to extinguish the remaining flames and save his home.

Later that Monday night, as the winds died down and a light drizzle hit the city, the Great Fire burned itself out. On Tuesday, Chicago started to rebuild. Now word spread throughout the ruined metropolis of how one determined man had fought the forces of destruction and won. It was an inspiring tale at a time when inspiration was needed.

The story quickly passed to the local newspapers and from there to the national press. In the years that followed, the "Triumph of Policeman

Policeman Bellinger's cottage on Hudson Avenue, a legendary survivor of the Great Fire. *Photo by the author.*

Bellinger" became a part of Chicago folklore. It was even reprinted in school textbooks. Each year on October 8, teachers would march their classes to the cottage on Hudson Avenue and tell their wide-eyed students how it had been saved by cider. Besides the Water Tower, this little frame house was the only building that had survived the disaster.

Then, one day in 1915, a little old white-haired lady appeared at the door of 2121 North Hudson Avenue. It was Mrs. Bellinger, back to visit the old homestead. She was invited in and looked around. Then she began to reminisce about the events of forty-four years before.

Yes, she said, her late husband had worked mightily to save the house, but her brother had also been there to help. After the fire, the Bellingers had sheltered twenty-one people in the tiny cottage. However, that business about using cider to put out the flames had been invented by a newspaper reporter with an overactive imagination. "We did have a barrel of cider in the basement," Mrs. Bellinger declared. "But we didn't use it because we were able to get enough water from the dugout across the street."

That destroyed one myth. And more recently, historians have determined that a few other wooden cottages on Cleveland Avenue also came through the fire. So the Bellinger house is not even unique as a survivor.

But it still makes a damn good story.

GLORIA SWANSON'S MANY CHICAGO HOMES

In June 1914, fifteen-year-old Gloria Swanson had just graduated from Lincoln Elementary School in Chicago. One day she tagged along when her Aunt Ingrid went to visit a friend at the Essanay Movie Studios in Uptown. By the end of that day, Gloria had been hired as an extra.

Swanson soon graduated to become an Essanay contract player. She appeared in a number of shorts and earned her first screen credits. In 1916, with the film industry consolidating in Hollywood, she left Chicago and moved to California. Her big break came in 1919, when she starred in Cecil B. DeMille's production *Don't Change Your Husband*. In the years that followed, she became the biggest female star of the silent screen.

Swanson's career stalled with the coming of sound in 1927. In 1950 she made a comeback in *Sunset Boulevard*, playing a role with which she could identify—a faded silent screen star. She continued performing, mostly on television, into the 1970s. Her last role was playing herself in the big-screen disaster epic *Airport 1975*. She died in 1983.

Those are the general facts of Gloria Swanson's professional life, and they are straightforward. Sorting out the facts of her Chicago years is more complicated.

Her father was Joseph T. Swanson, a professional soldier. Her mother was the former Adelaide Klanowski. The couple married in 1898. Their only child, Gloria May Josephine Swanson, was born on March 27, 1899. Like Walt Disney, another famous film figure born in Chicago around the same time, Gloria Swanson had no official birth certificate. This has led to some confusion about her birthplace.

In her 1980 autobiography titled *Swanson on Swanson*, Gloria noted that she was born on the second floor of 341 Grace Street in Chicago. After the city's address numbers were changed in 1909, the house at that number became 2017 West Grace Street. Yet there are no contemporary records showing a Grace Street connection to Swanson's family. How Gloria came up with that address is unknown.

Steven Michael Shearer's exhaustive 2013 biography *Gloria Swanson: The Ultimate Star* offers a different location. He has Swanson's birthplace at 150 Seminary Avenue, based on the 1900 U.S. Census. Unfortunately, Shearer misread the census sheet. The Swanson family residence is actually listed there as 885 Seminary Avenue, an address confirmed by the "Joseph T.

The brick three-flat where movie star Gloria Swanson was (probably) born, now in the shadow of Wrigley Field's scoreboard. *Photo by the author.*

Swanson" entry in both the 1900 and 1901 city directories. That address is 3124 North Seminary Avenue today.

Yet another story claims that Swanson was actually born in a cottage on Grace just east of Clark Street, but she somehow got the address wrong. Later that cottage was supposedly moved to 3710 North Kenmore Avenue, just behind the left field fence at Wrigley Field, where it stands today. This spot is endorsed in oral history passed down by generations of firemen at the firehouse around the corner.

As it happens, the firemen have the street right but the wrong building. The 1899 city directory has Gloria's father residing at 1316 Osgood Street, which became 3703 North Kenmore Avenue. The building there today matches the photo in Swanson's autobiography. So it would seem that this was her birthplace.

As Swanson herself said, her family moved around a lot when she was a child. The 1902 and 1903 city directories list her father at 340 Center Street, which is now 502 West Armitage Avenue. Then, for three years beginning in 1904, the family lived at 1122 Otto Street. Today, this is 1238 West Henderson Street. A few blocks away is Hawthorne Elementary School, which Gloria remembered attending.

In 1907 Joseph Swanson was transferred to Key West, Florida. During his posting there, his wife and daughter divided their time between living with him and living with relatives in Chicago. They followed the same procedure when Joseph was later reassigned to Puerto Rico. Most likely they spent their Chicago months with Gloria's maternal uncle at 1615 West Foster Avenue.

Finally, in 1915, Gloria Swanson earned her own entry in the Chicago City Directory. She was then living at 4215 North Leavitt Street. Her profession is listed as "actress."

The Vice President from Evanston

"Once upon a time, there were two brothers. One of them went to sea. The other became vice president of the United States. Neither of them was ever heard from again."

That was an old vaudeville joke, and it always got a laugh. It was true enough. Charles Gates Dawes was our thirtieth vice president, and he lived in Illinois. But unless you are from Evanston, you probably never heard of the man.

The son of a Civil War general who later served in Congress, Dawes was born in Ohio in 1865. He studied law in Cincinnati and then set up a legal practice in Nebraska. In 1894 he moved to Illinois. Becoming active in banking and Republican politics, he was appointed to a sub-cabinet position in the McKinley administration. Later he made an unsuccessful run for the U.S. Senate. He bought the house at 225 Greenwood Street in Evanston in 1909.

During World War I, Dawes was a brigadier general in charge of procurement. He was called before a Congressional committee investigating waste. The questions got heated, and he finally exploded. "Hell-and-Maria, we weren't keeping a set of books!" he yelled. "We were trying to win the war!" The newspapers loved it, and forever after, the dignified Dawes was nicknamed Hell-and-Maria Dawes. (We will pause here to consider what Dawes meant by the phrase "Hell-and-Maria." Does anyone cuss like that today?)

After the war, Dawes again went to Washington, this time for the Harding administration, as the first director of the newly established Bureau of the Budget. This put him in charge of German reparations. The Treaty of Versailles required Germany to pay billions of dollars to the victorious Allies. With their economy in ruins, the Germans were having trouble making payments.

The Evanston home of Vice President Charles Gates Dawes. Hell-and-Maria! *Photo by the author.*

So, Dawes came up with the Dawes Plan, part of which worked something like this: (1) The United States loans money to Germany; (2) Germany uses the money to pay reparations to Britain and France; and (3) Britain and France send the money back to the United States to pay their war debt. Unless you are an international banker, this may sound like an odd way of doing business. But the plan did win Dawes the Nobel Peace Prize.

On a lighter note, smokers might be interested to learn that Dawes popularized the Dawes Pipe. If you've never seen one, think of the letter *P*. Now rotate it ninety degrees to the right, and you'll get the idea.

Dawes became vice president in a peculiar way. In 1924 President Calvin Coolidge was looking for a running mate from a swing state. Former Illinois governor Frank Lowden was actually nominated by the Republican National Convention. Then Lowden shocked everyone by turning down the spot. Senator William Borah of Idaho was approached, and he also declined. After considering and rejecting Commerce Secretary Herbert Hoover, the party mandarins settled on Dawes. He agreed, Coolidge agreed and the deed was done. In keeping with the custom of the time, Dawes delivered his acceptance speech from the porch of the house on Greenwood Street.

The Coolidge-Dawes ticket won a landslide victory. After that, the two men didn't get along. Matters were not helped when the vice president missed a crucial tie-breaking vote in the Senate, and one of the president's cabinet nominees was rejected. Dawes was back at his hotel at the time, taking a nap.

Dawes was never seriously considered as a presidential candidate. When Coolidge declined to run again in 1928, Hoover won the nomination, thought about keeping Dawes as his running mate and then picked someone else. After Hoover was elected, he did reward the outgoing veep with a plum diplomatic appointment as ambassador to Great Britain.

Dawes returned to Evanston and banking after his ambassadorship. He died in 1951. Under terms of his will, his house eventually passed to Northwestern University. Today, the Dawes House is a museum operated by the Evanston Historical Society.

There is one more bit of trivia. Dawes was a self-taught pianist and composer. During the 1950s, Carl Sigman took Dawes's "Melody in A Major," added lyrics and came up with a song titled "It's All in the Game." In 1958 the Tommy Edwards recording of the work reached number one on the *Billboard* chart.

What would Charles Gates Dawes have said to that? Probably "Hell-and-Maria!"

THE LEANING TOWER OF NILES

The Leaning Tower of Pisa has been leaning in that northern Italian city since the twelfth century. Closer to home, at 6300 West Touhy Avenue, Chicagoans can visit the Leaning Tower of Niles.

The story begins in 1931 with Robert Ilg, owner of an electric air ventilation company, who was planning a park for his employees. The park needed a water tank for its swimming pool. According to the usual story, Ilg decided to house the tank in a Leaning Tower replica as a tribute to Galileo Galilei, the Renaissance scientist who'd carried out experiments in the Italian original.

The Pisa tower leans because it was built on sandy ground—the tilt was a mistake that was never corrected. Ilg hired a San Francisco engineering firm to construct his tower with a ready-made tilt. To ensure that the angle would stay constant, the engineers laid a concrete foundation.

Ilg's tower was completed in 1934. It was ninety-four feet tall and twenty-eight feet in diameter, a half-scale model of the Italian tower. The tilt was 7.4 degrees. Five bells were hung in the tower. Unlike the marble original, the Niles version was constructed of steel and concrete.

For the next quarter century, the park and the tower were enjoyed by the employees of the Ilg Hot Air Electric Ventilating Company. During that time, the YMCA began using the property. In 1958 Y-workers raised more than $54,000 to help renovate the interior of the tower. The Skokie Valley YMCA had established its headquarters at the site, and the money was also used to build an athletic field, skating rink and campgrounds.

After Robert Ilg's death in 1960, his heirs gave the tower and the surrounding land to the YMCA. The tower was to be maintained for a period of ninety-nine years, with a minimum of $500 spent each year on upkeep. In 1964 a new facility opened on the property called the Leaning Tower YMCA.

Meanwhile, Ilg's monument was attracting a special sort of notoriety. The site was just down Touhy Avenue from O'Hare Airport. For many years, travelers on layover would hop in a cab to Niles, snap a few pictures at the tower and be back at the terminal in little over an hour. Tightened airport security ended these jaunts.

Of course, word had filtered back to Pisa that some crazy American had built his own Leaning Tower. So, when Niles officials began pursuing a Sister Cities agreement with Pisa during the 1960s, the Italian city was leery. Why should a prosperous metropolis of 100,000 people join with a "grape-

The Niles version of Pisa's Leaning Tower. *Photo by the author.*

stomping village" in the wilderness? After Pisan officials finally visited Niles in 1991, the Sister Cities pact was signed.

The Italian city was having structural problems with its eight-hundred-year-old tower then. The much younger American replica was having its own problems, and public access to the interior had to be closed. In 1995 the Village of Niles came to the rescue by leasing the tower from the YMCA. A new round of repairs and renovation began. The concrete was fixed and new lights installed on each of the eight floors, while four fountains and a thirty-foot reflecting pool were added to the grounds. The total cost was $1.2 million. The landmark appeared to be saved.

Two decades passed. In 2014 a new study determined that the Niles tower needed further repairs, with an estimated price tag of $600,000. Pisa had spent nearly $30 million to restore its own tower, so Niles officials were willing to undertake the necessary work on what had become a symbol of the village. The village purchased the tower from the YMCA for a token payment of $10 in 2017. By that time, about $750,000 had been spent on the latest round of work.

And then there are those bells. The same five have hung in the tower since its dedication, although they have been rung only on special occasions. During the 2017 renovations, an outside consultant determined that the bells were among the oldest in the United States, one of them dating from 1623. How they found their way into Robert Ilg's Niles Leaning Tower is a mystery.

HILLARY'S HOME

For many Park Ridge residents, the 2016 presidential election focused attention on the modest two-story brick home at 235 North Wisner Street. This is the house where Hillary Rodham Clinton grew up.

A number of sources—including the National Portrait Gallery—have said that Hillary is a Park Ridge native. She was actually born at Edgewater Hospital in Chicago in 1947 and lived nearby at 5722 North Winthrop Avenue until she was three. The Rodham family then moved to Park Ridge.

Her parents were Hugh Rodham and the former Dorothy Howell. Hugh was in the textile business, and Dorothy was a homemaker. Hillary was their first child. She was later joined by two brothers. The Rodhams were a typical, suburban, upper-middle-class household of the baby boom years.

Hillary attended Field Elementary School and later Emerson Junior High School, graduating in 1961. She then moved on to Maine Township High School. But the baby boom was really booming, so in 1964, the district opened a new high school, Maine South. Hillary transferred there for her senior year.

If you had to put her in a category, Hillary would be one of the Smart Girls. She always ranked near the top of her class, and the teachers liked her. At the same time, she was not an introvert bookworm. Her list of extracurricular activities was extensive and varied—student council, variety show, Girls' Athletic Association, speech and debate, the class newspaper and so on. Her classmates voted her the "Girl Most Likely to Succeed."

Like any high school student, she had some setbacks. She ran for student council president and lost. Her application to become an astronaut received the polite reply that NASA did not accept girls.

Hillary Rodham graduated from Maine South in 1965 and left Park Ridge to attend Wellesley College. By the Wellesley graduation four years later, the onetime Republican Goldwater Girl had now become a Democrat. Hillary then went to Yale Law School and met Bill Clinton. The rest is history—and for once, that phrase in not a cliché.

Meanwhile, back in Park Ridge, the Rodham family was still living on Wisner Street. They sold the house in 1987 and moved to Arkansas to be closer to Hillary and Bill and their granddaughter, Chelsea. When Hillary entered the national spotlight during her husband's 1992 presidential campaign, at first Park Ridge officials didn't know where she had lived. But many of her old friends were still around, happy to point out the house and share their memories.

First Lady, U.S. senator, secretary of state, presidential candidate—the house in Park Ridge where Hillary Rodham Clinton grew up. *Photo by the author.*

Hillary returned to Park Ridge as First Lady on October 27, 1997, the day after her fiftieth birthday. Joined by her mother and two brothers—her father had died a few years earlier—she made a nostalgic tour of her old neighborhood. Nearly five hundred people were on hand to greet her when she arrived at the Wisner Street house. She had lunch at the First United Methodist Church and visited Field School, where the children sang "Happy Birthday." The Park Ridge City Council proclaimed a "Hillary Rodham Clinton Day."

No one thought that Hillary would fade into obscurity once her tenure as First Lady ended. She built her own political career and stayed in the news. And Park Ridge remembered her too. The intersection of Wisner and Elm Streets was officially designated Rodham Corner. Both Park Ridge high schools engaged in a friendly rivalry regarding which had the better claim for Hillary as an alumna. Maine South claimed the privilege because of her graduation in 1965. Her original high school—now called Maine East—countered by pointing out that they had her for three years, not just one.

Hillary visited Park Ridge as a U.S. senator in 2003, doing a TV interview at her favorite high school restaurant. She came back again during her 2016 presidential run for a closed-door fundraiser at the Pickwick Theatre. As that campaign moved on, there were proposals to rename a local park in Hillary's honor or to convert her childhood home into a museum. A few boosters talked up the suburb as the future site of a presidential library.

The results of the 2016 election have put an end to that last project. At this writing, the house on Wisner Street is a private residence.

BRING 'EM BACK ALIVE

When he died in 1950, Frank Buck was known throughout the world. Buck was a hunter who didn't kill animals. Rather, his slogan was "Bring 'Em Back Alive"—and that's what he did, capturing exotic beasts for zoos, circuses and the movies. He was also a showman who publicized his adventures in numerous books and his own documentary films.

But before Frank Buck became famous, he lived in Chicago. His onetime home is located on the far Northwest Side, at 6814 West Ardmore Avenue.

Buck was a Texan, born in Gainesville in 1884 and raised in Dallas. In 1900 he hired on to accompany a load of cattle being shipped to the Chicago Stock Yards and then decided to stay on in the city to seek his fortune. He moved through a series of short-lived jobs until he found work as a flunky at the Virginia Hotel on the Near North Side. Bright and ambitious, he soon was promoted to bell captain.

On July 17, 1901, Frank Buck made the front page of the *Chicago Tribune*. He had married a celebrity. "Amy Leslie Weds a 'Bell'" the headline read. Amy Leslie was the well-respected drama critic of the *Chicago Daily News*, one of the few women in the country holding such a prestigious post. Her new husband, described as "big, handsome, and tactful," was Frank Buck. The paper noted that "the dark-haired [Buck] had not carried ice water to her apartments many times before she became interested in him."

The couple had been involved in a discreet romance for several months. Now Frank had quit his job, and they had eloped and been married in St. Joseph, Michigan. Amy told the license clerk that she was forty-five, and Frank said he was twenty-three. Their actual ages were forty-one and seventeen.

Writing in his 1941 autobiography, a few years after Amy's death, Frank disclosed that Amy had proposed to him. He had initially turned her down because of their age difference and their "vastly different stations in life." But Amy had persisted. "You are on your way up," she'd told him. "I can help you."

Frank and Amy set up housekeeping in a North Side apartment. Frank worked in the music publishing business and then moved into the management end of a vaudeville circuit. Amy continued writing for the *Daily News*.

At heart, Frank was still a country boy. He liked the bright lights and city life well enough yet was looking for something more. A few years into his marriage, he bought a house in the Norwood Park neighborhood, on the outskirts of the city. Amy wasn't thrilled by the move. Still, she went along with it.

Part of the attraction of the Norwood Park house was its huge lot. Frank took hammer and nails in hand and built an aviary on the property to collect birds. He began reading scientific treatises about animals. He made regular expeditions to Lincoln Park Zoo for firsthand observation, all the while peppering the staff with questions. He was gradually forming a plan.

Frank wrote that Amy was "the most brilliant and cultured woman I have ever known" and credited her with smoothing out his rough edges. Although he says they were happy for many years, he also said, "I think that from the very beginning Amy had never really believed that our marriage could last."

The turning point came in 1913, when Frank won $3,500 in a poker game. He used the money to travel to South America and begin collecting birds. With the profits from that venture, he moved into the business that would eventually become his life's work. Frank and Amy divorced that year, by all accounts amicably.

During the 1980s, *Bring 'Em Back Alive*, a fictionalized TV series based on Buck's exploits, lasted a single season. More recently, an anthology drawn from his writings was published under the same title. Today, the Frank Buck Zoo in Gainesville continues his legacy.

After his divorce from Amy, Frank Buck never again lived in Chicago. City directories list his Norwood Park residence as 265 Crescent Avenue. The address became 6814 West Crescent Avenue when the street numbers were changed, and it is now 6814 West Ardmore Avenue. Frank and Amy's former house is a private residence.

CHICAGO'S OLDEST HOUSE?

The 1836 Henry B. Clarke House, at 1855 South Indiana Avenue, is often cited as Chicago's oldest building. The city has spent much time and money developing it as a historic site, and the location just south of the Loop has made it a magnet for tourists. But out on the far Northwest Side, at 5624 North Newark Avenue, there is an even older house.

Mark Noble was an Englishman. In 1823 his son, John, immigrated to America. John liked what he saw and finally convinced the rest of the family to join him. Mark, his wife and their three other children arrived at the little settlement near the mouth of the Chicago River in 1831.

The family spent their first winter in the old Kinzie cabin. While living there Mark Noble helped organize the town's first Methodist congregation. The next year he bought a tract across the river on the south bank and settled into a shanty on the property. Sometime during this period he went into a partnership operating a steam-powered sawmill on the Des Plaines River. That started him looking for a homesite closer to his business.

In 1833 Noble purchased 160 acres of timber land a dozen miles northwest of Chicago from a man identified as "the half-breed Jean Mirandeau." Noble also claimed additional land in Jefferson Township for a total of 600 acres and built a single-story twenty-five-by-thirty-foot frame house on the Waukegan Road.

But Mark Noble's life as a timber entrepreneur and gentleman farmer didn't last long. He died in 1839. His son, Mark Jr., lived in the house for a few years afterward before moving on.

The Noble family eventually sold off the property, and it passed through a series of owners until Thomas Seymour bought the home in 1868. Seymour was part of the company developing the new village of Norwood Park in the area. Since he had a large family and live-in servants, he immediately topped off the original Noble building with a second floor, as well as adding on a new two-story wing to the north of it.

Seymour used the property with its expanded house as a country farm. He planted a vineyard and an orchard with more than a thousand apple and cherry trees. For a while he raised blooded short-horn cattle.

Chicago annexed Norwood Park in 1893. Waukegan Road became Newark Avenue. Thomas Seymour died in 1915, and the land to the north and west of his homestead was subdivided. The house itself was sold again.

The new owner was concert pianist Stuart Crippen. He added electricity and indoor plumbing, converting the house into a year-round residence. It remained in the Crippen family for more than seventy years. As the children grew up and got married, the house was divided into separate flats.

In 1987 the Crippens put the old homestead up for sale. Developers had their eyes on the 1.7-acre property, but the Norwood Park Historical Society beat them out. The purchase price was $285,000.

With aid from various sources, the historical society began renovating what was now known as the Noble-Seymour-Crippen House. The goal was to

The 1833 Noble-Seymour-Crippen House on Newark Avenue. *Photo by the author.*

restore an early twentieth-century appearance. While the work was going on, the original provenance was confirmed—the southern section of the house dated from 1833, making it the oldest building within the Chicago city limits.

The Noble-Seymour-Crippen House became an official city landmark in 1988. In 2000 it was placed in the National Register of Historic Places. The house has even made it into the movies, appearing in the John Goodman film *The Babe*. Today, the Norwood Park Historical Society operates it as a museum.

There is still a bit of rivalry with the Henry B. Clarke House. Although that building has been moved a few times from the original site, its partisans note that Clarke's home was within the city limits when Chicago was incorporated in 1837. They dismiss Mark Noble's home as a farmhouse that happened to survive long enough to be annexed by an expanding city decades later.

Both homes are fun to visit. Then make your own choice on which one deserves the title of "Chicago's Oldest."

ROBINSON FAMILY GRAVES

If you are driving down East River Road, along another of Cook County's forest preserves, make a stop at the pullout just north of Lawrence Avenue. Follow the paved footpath a few hundred feet into the woods. You have just found the Robinson family grave site.

Much like the history of early Chicago, the story of the family patriarch is liberally salted with legend. Alexander Robinson was probably born near the Straits of Mackinac in 1787, the son of a Scottish trader and a French-Chippewa woman (some sources say French-Ottawa). His tribal name was Chee-chee-pin-quay, which translates as "blinking eye"—he was said to have had a facial tic.

During his teens Robinson became friends with John Kinzie. By 1812 he had followed Kinzie to Chicago, built a large house on the south branch of the river and become active in the fur trade. That summer Robinson helped rescue Captain Heald and other Americans after the Battle of Fort Dearborn.

Robinson returned to Chicago after the fort was rebuilt in 1815. Besides his ongoing work in the fur trade, he found employment as an interpreter. He also opened one of the settlement's first taverns, although he himself was a teetotaler. Robinson could not read or write, but he kept track of his business accounts through his own system of printed characters.

The details of Robinson's family life are confused. Some sources say that he was first married to a Menominee woman named Cynthia Sahsos. Then, in 1826, Robinson married Catherine Chevalier, daughter of a Potawatomi chief. Yet another source declares that Robinson never bothered to divorce his first wife and that Cynthia "retained a position within the household" after Alexander and Catherine married.

In 1829, through some convenient maneuvering, Robinson became one of the Potawatomi chiefs. When the Black Hawk War broke out a few years later, he used his influence to keep the Potawatomi tribe from joining the conflict. Robinson also helped negotiate the two treaties in which the native tribes ceded their local lands. The federal government recognized his services by granting him a 1,280-acre reserve on the Des Plaines River. He also received a lump-sum cash payment and an annual pension.

Although his colleague Billy Caldwell moved out of the area, Robinson decided to settle on his land. He built a house near the banks of the Des Plaines and eventually raised a family of twelve children. One of the early city directories lists him as a "farmer." From time to time, history buffs and curiosity seekers trekked out to the homestead, and Alexander Robinson delighted in telling the familiar old stories. He died at his home on April 22, 1872, and was buried on the property.

Members of the Robinson family continued to live on the homestead after Alexander's death. At various times, portions of the reserve were sold off. Questions arose whether the sales were legally executed. At length, the

The path off East River Road leading to the Robinson family homestead site and graves. *Photo by the author.*

Robinson heirs became involved in a dispute with the Cook County Board of Commissioners, which wanted the land for a forest preserve. The result was a court decision conveying the land to the county but guaranteeing Alexander Robinson's descendants the right to continue their residence. The old homestead was destroyed in a 1955 fire, after which the last heirs vacated the property.

By then eleven members of the Robinson family had been laid to rest in the family plot. Because of vandalism, the county removed the headstones and placed them in storage. A large boulder with information about the family was placed nearby. The graves themselves remained unmarked.

In 2016 a forest preserve employee came across the long-forgotten headstones. Robinson family descendants were located and filed the necessary paperwork to reclaim them. Portions of the stones had crumbled away during their decades in storage. They are now stored more accessibly in the Schiller Park Public Library. The library was chosen because it stands on what was once part of Alexander Robinson's land.

Today, the informational boulder is still in place in the forest preserve. The individual graves are still unmarked, although there has been discussion about erecting new headstones. The homestead site itself is deeper in the forest, close to the river. Local ghost hunters claim that the property is haunted.

The Ground 'L'

The Loop elevated line has become a tourist attraction. Major American cities no longer have iron railroad trestles running over streets in their central business districts. This remnant of nineteenth-century transit is distinctly Chicago, the way the cable cars are distinctly San Francisco. Yet there is another feature of the Chicago 'L' that most visitors ignore: the ground-level sections.

The original South Side 'L' opened in 1892. Soon other lines on iron trestles followed. But building trestles cost serious money. When the transit companies wanted to extend their original lines into sparsely settled areas, they simply laid the tracks on the ground. Over the course of a century, much of this surface trackage was grade-separated. Today, four CTA routes continue to have some ground-level service.

The Yellow Line was known at various times as the Niles Center Line or the Skokie Swift. The line operates on the right-of-way of the old North Shore interurban railroad, from Howard Street station west and north to a terminal at Dempster Street in Skokie. From East Prairie Road west to Dempster, the trains run at grade.

The Purple Line was originally the Evanston Line, running at ground level from Howard Street station to a northern terminal at Linden Avenue in Wilmette. Most of the line was later elevated. However, the final half mile to Linden is still on the ground.

The Pink Line was originally the Douglas Park Line. At one time, trains on the outer portion of the line descended from the elevated structure at Kildare Avenue in the city and operated at grade for nearly three miles, to a western terminal at Oak Park Avenue in Berwyn. During the 1950s the line was cut back to its current terminal at 54th Avenue in Cicero. Today, the Pink Line's grade-level trackage covers a little more than one mile.

The Brown Line is a special case and the major point of our interest. The outer mile of this line operates at grade-level in the middle of an alley. Unlike the ground sections of the other three routes, this one runs through one of the most densely populated neighborhoods of Chicago.

Today's Brown Line began as the Ravenswood branch of the Northwestern Elevated Railroad. In May 1907, service was opened on the branch from the Roscoe-Sheffield junction west and north to a terminal at Western Avenue near Wilson. As required by city franchise, the trains ran on an elevated trestle.

West of the terminal, a large parcel of land stretching to Kimball Avenue was being developed by the Northwest Land Association. The company knew that train service would boost the sale of its lots, so a deal was struck between

Along the outer mile of the Brown Line 'L,' where trains run through an alley on the ground. *Photo by the author.*

the developer and the railroad. Northwest Land gave Northwestern Elevated a free right-of-way through its property to Kimball. Since this part of the line was being built entirely on private land, no city franchise was needed and the tracks could be laid at ground level. Construction would be quicker and cheaper.

There were also some bonuses. Northwest Land agreed to share the construction costs of two stations. And for three years after the extension was built, the developer would pay for all operating losses.

Before 1907 was over, trains were running on the extension. At first there was only a shuttle car between Kimball and Western. In little more than a year, traffic had increased so dramatically that the shuttle was replaced by through service from Kimball to the Loop. Within a decade, the outer mile of the line was surrounded by newly built apartment buildings, justifying Northwest Land's concessions to Northwestern Elevated. Today, the ground-level tracks have six crossings and four stations. Despite the obvious safety concerns, there are very few accidents.

In 1958 plans were unveiled to lower the tracks in an open-cut arrangement at some future date. The idea was popular with neighborhood residents, and similar proposals are floated from time to time. However, in more recent years, CTA has spent millions of dollars to extend the station platforms on the entire Brown Line, including the outer four. So it's a good bet that 'L' trains will continue rumbling on the ground through the alleys of Albany Park for another century.

CHICAGO'S SHORTEST STREET

If you know your Chicago trivia, you know that Western Avenue is the city's longest street. From Howard Street to 119th Street, Western runs in a straight line for 23.5 miles. But what is Chicago's shortest street? That has been subject to debate for a long time.

When I was a teenager in the early 1960s, a friend told me that Somerset Avenue, a street in his neighborhood, was the shortest street in Chicago. Somerset is a little lane running southwest from the intersection of Nagle and Avondale Avenues (5700 north at 6400 west) to Northcott Avenue. One day, my friend and I paced off the tiny street. It was something like one hundred feet long.

Somerset Avenue originally ran past Northcott, all the way to Natoma Avenue. During the 1930s, construction of the Taft High School campus closed off this part of Somerset. All that was left was the tiny stub at the northern end.

A few months after we'd paced off Somerset, I discovered that we'd been wasting our time. Somerset was not the shortest street in Chicago. According to the *Chicago Daily News*, Ziegfeld Court was.

Ziegfeld Court was named for showman Florenz Ziegfeld Jr., a Chicago native. This mini-street was actually an alley, located next to the Ziegfeld Theater, on the north side of Van Buren Street just east of Wabash Avenue. The official dimensions of Ziegfeld Court were 76.4 feet long and 10 feet wide.

I'm not sure when Ziegfeld Court became Chicago's shortest street. I suspect that the little alley got its name—and ascended to the status of an official street—when the theater was built during the 1920s. In any event, the city vacated Ziegfeld Court in 1970. The street was sold to Continental Assurance for $151,300. That works out to $198 per square foot, reportedly the highest price ever received by the City of Chicago for a public thoroughfare. The CNA Center now occupies the site.

Some people didn't seem to get the news of the sale. For many years afterward, various sources still claimed that Ziegfeld Court was Chicago's shortest street. In 2008, the Forgotten Chicago website tried to clear up the confusion with an article titled "Tiny Streets." Instead of using physical measurements, the length of the different streets was determined by their address points—what a layperson might call house numbers.

Using that criterion, Chicago's shortest street was McDermott Street, a stub off Archer Avenue in the Bridgeport neighborhood. The street is officially listed at 1400 west, from 2928 to 2936 south. That's eight address

Bay Court, Chicago's shortest street. *Photo by the author.*

points. Hoey Street, a few blocks away, was ranked the city's second-shortest, with ten address points.

Since the city's address point system can be inconsistent, I decided to take my own readings. In 2012, nearly a half century after I had paced off Somerset Avenue, I paced off both McDermott and Hoey, from the curb lines of the nearest intersecting streets. Based on these unscientific measurements, it appeared that Hoey was shorter than McDermott. I posted the results on my blog.

That opened up a discussion. The 1988 book *Streetwise Chicago* listed the city's shortest street as Longmeadow Avenue at 31.6 feet long. However, Longmeadow is actually a Lincolnwood street, located north of the Devon Avenue border with Chicago. Its name changes after it passes Devon. That 31.6-foot stub on the Chicago side of Devon is actually part of Lenox Avenue.

In recent years, various parcels of the city's industrial land have been redeveloped for residential use. The planners of these subdivisions often depart from the existing street grid. It's a form of artistic self-expression.

As I write this in 2019, the little champ of Chicago mini-streets is in a new residential tract just west of the Chicago River, off Belmont Avenue. Using precise Geographic Information System measurement, it would seem that the city's shortest street is Bay Court (2710 west at 3300 north) with a total length of 127.52 feet. Nearby Pier Court is the second-shortest, at 128.88 feet.

Perhaps we will be seeing more of these boutique streets in the future. And Chicago developers may even want to set a new record. According to the record book, the shortest street in the world is Ebenezer Place in Wick, County Caithness, in Scotland—6.9 feet long.

RED EMMA'S HIDEOUT

A while back, I wrote a book titled *On This Day in Chicago History*, which described a local event that happened on each day of the calendar year. I already knew what the big national news story was on September 11, 2001. But instead of researching Chicago's reaction to the 9/11 terrorist attacks, I decided to find out what the big local news story was exactly one hundred years earlier, on September 11, 1901.

Strangely enough, the headlines that day proclaimed that the hunt for America's most wanted terrorist had ended here in Chicago, in a building on Sheffield Avenue. The alleged terrorist was Emma Goldman. She was accused of conspiring to murder the president of the United States.

On September 6, in Buffalo, President William McKinley was shot and seriously wounded. The gunman was an anarchist named Leon Czolgosz. He told police that he'd been inspired to his deed by Emma Goldman.

At thirty-two, the Russian-born Goldman was known to be an organizer and promoter of radical-left causes. She had become an anarchist after the unjust hangings in the aftermath of the Haymarket Riot. Czolgosz had heard her speak in Chicago the previous July. The two had talked for perhaps a half hour and then gone their separate ways.

Chicago officials believed that the plot to kill the president had been hatched right here. Six of Goldman's associates were arrested. Goldman was thought to be in St. Louis. Before police could act on this information, they received a new tip—Red Emma was on her way to Chicago!

Goldman arrived by train, but the cops missed her. Meanwhile, they'd staked out some of her known haunts. On the evening of September 9, a woman fitting Goldman's description was seen entering an apartment building at what's now 2126 North Sheffield Avenue. She remained inside throughout the night and into the next day.

Shortly before noon, the police moved in. The suspect was in a flat on the third floor. While one officer knocked at the door, another climbed in through the window. They found a tiny, mild-looking woman sitting peacefully in a rocking chair, smiling at them.

At first the woman denied she was Emma Goldman. That didn't last long. Admitting her identity, Goldman went quietly along to police headquarters. In less than an hour, newspaper extras were on the street, announcing the capture of the most dangerous woman in America.

Goldman faced questioning from the chief of police, a dozen detectives and Mayor Carter Harrison Jr.—his father, the first Mayor Harrison, had

Front-page portrait heralding the arrest of "Anarchy's High Priestess," Emma Goldman. *From the* Chicago Tribune, *September 11, 1901.*

been killed by an assassin. She remained calm and polite throughout the lengthy interrogation. She even joked about fooling the cops who had come to arrest her at the Sheffield Avenue flat and how the city would be giving her a free dinner today.

Questioned about the McKinley shooting, Goldman refused to condemn it. Instead, she said that the president himself was "too insignificant" to be murdered, that he was only a tool in the hand of the monopolists. As for Czolgosz, she had met him only that one time. She hadn't been in Buffalo since the middle of August. She wasn't part of any conspiracy.

Goldman saw her arrest as an opportunity to get her views before the public and talked about them at length. She readily agreed to pose for a *Chicago Tribune* photographer. A good portrait might help the police find her more quickly the next time!

McKinley died on September 14. Six weeks later, Czolgosz was executed. No evidence was found linking Goldman or her associates to the crime, and they were all released. Goldman herself was deported from the United States during the "Red Scare" of 1919. When she died in Canada in 1940, her remains were returned to Chicago. Her grave is at Forest Home Cemetery in Forest Park.

In 2014 the Canadian TV series *Murdoch Mysteries* (aka *The Artful Detective*) aired an episode about Goldman's arrest in the wake of the McKinley shooting. For dramatic purposes, they moved the setting to Toronto. The show is one of my favorites, and it was a well-done episode. But if you want to see where it really happened, you have to go to Sheffield Avenue.

THE NAZI SABOTEUR ON FREMONT STREET

A few blocks from Emma Goldman's 1901 hideout, there is another forgotten Lincoln Park landmark. The apartment building at 2234 North Fremont Street has been renovated, but it's still the same building that was there on June 27, 1942. On that morning, Herbie Haupt walked out the front door and into history.

Haupt was twenty-two years old. He got into his new Pontiac convertible, drove a block south to Webster and then turned right. At the 'L' underpass, another car forced him to the curb. Three FBI agents emerged from the second car and placed him under arrest. He was charged with being a German spy.

The United States had been at war with Nazi Germany for about seven months. Haupt was part of an eight-man team that had been dropped off the Atlantic coast by submarine a few days earlier. Their mission, known as Operation Pastorius, was to blow up American defense plants and transportation facilities. The plan had been personally approved by German dictator Adolf Hitler.

Herbert Hans Haupt was born in the German port city of Stettin in 1919. His family moved to Chicago when he was a boy. Herbie became an American citizen at age ten, when his parents were naturalized. He graduated from Waters Elementary School, moved on to Amundsen High School and then transferred to Lane Tech. Before dropping out of Lane, he was a cadet in ROTC.

Haupt found work at the Simpson Optical factory. In the summer of 1941, he set off for Mexico. According to another German-born young man who went with him, the trip was planned as a short vacation. Other sources say that the two men quit their jobs. After a series of adventures that took them through Japan, Herbie and his buddy wound up in German territory on December 11, 1941—the day their native country declared war on their adopted country.

Germany still considered the two Chicagoans to be German citizens. Haupt's traveling companion wound up in the German army. Herbie was a different case. He spoke near-perfect English, was familiar with America and American customs and could easily blend in. He was a perfect fit for the sabotage mission. Herbie later claimed to have joined the plot only so he could get back home to Chicago.

The eight men recruited for Operation Pastorius were all German natives who'd lived in the United States. They underwent three weeks of intensive training in bomb-making and other useful skills. Early in June 1942, they were landed on American soil.

The team had been split into two four-man groups. One unit came ashore in Long Island and the other in Florida. Soon after arriving, two men from the first group decided to abandon the mission. One of these men contacted the FBI. The FBI began tracking the others.

Haupt was part of the Florida group. Along with another man, he took a train to Chicago. The two of them were supposed to settle in and prepare for the next phase of the mission. Haupt went to his parents' apartment on Fremont Street.

Did they wonder why Herbie suddenly appeared after being gone nearly a year? They didn't ask, he didn't tell. He seemed to have plenty of money.

The Fremont Street home of ROTC cadet turned Nazi saboteur Herbie Haupt. *Photo by the author.*

He bought a new car. He began dating a neighborhood girl. Then the FBI nabbed him.

President Franklin D. Roosevelt ordered the eight terrorists be tried by military tribunal. Their lawyers attempted to get the cases moved to civilian courts. In a landmark ruling known as *Ex parte Quirin*, the U.S. Supreme Court denied the appeal. The accused were classified under the laws of warfare as "unlawful combatants."

All eight men were quickly found guilty by the tribunals and sentenced to death. Roosevelt commuted the executions of the two Germans who'd dropped out of the plot, giving them prison time instead. The other six—including U.S. citizen Herbie Haupt—died in the electric chair on August 8, 1942.

In recent years, the Supreme Court ruling in the Nazi terrorist case has become part of the discussion about the Guantanamo Prison detainees. Historians still debate the motivations behind Herbie Haupt's actions. The building on Fremont Street where he spent his last hours of freedom is privately owned.

THE TOMB IN THE PARK

If you've wandered around Lincoln Park behind the Chicago History Museum, you've seen the squat stone structure bearing the word "Couch." Most people think it is part of the museum. Don't be fooled by the location. This is a real mausoleum.

The south end of today's Lincoln Park was once Chicago City Cemetery. In 1837, when the cemetery was established, the site was far removed from the little settlement near the mouth of the Chicago River, making it a good place to put the deceased. The more prosperous Chicagoans constructed mausoleums. This is where the "Couch" comes in—Ira Couch, to be precise.

Couch was born in 1806 in Saratoga County, New York. At sixteen he apprenticed as a tailor and later opened his own shop. In 1836 Ira visited Chicago along with his elder brother, James. The brothers liked the bustling new town and decided to stay. They first operated a general store, unsuccessfully. James had worked as a hotel clerk, so in 1837 they decided to go into that business. They secured a lease on a run-down frame inn at Lake and Dearborn Streets, spruced things up and reopened it as the Tremont House. Two years later, the building burned down. Undaunted, the Couch brothers rebuilt. The second Tremont House lasted ten years, until a fire destroyed it too.

Again the brothers rebuilt. This time they used stone. The third Tremont House boasted 260 rooms. The hotel gained a reputation as the city's finest, the preferred accommodations for the rich and famous who stopped in Chicago. The venture did so well that Ira was able to retire in 1853 at the age of forty-seven, leaving James to carry on with the hotel.

Now Ira's health began to deteriorate. Early in 1857 he set off with his family for a winter vacation in Cuba. At Havana he came down with a fever. He died there on February 28, 1857, barely fifty years old.

Ira's body was shipped back to Chicago. John Van Osdel, the city's first professional architect, was commissioned to design a suitable mausoleum for the Couch family. The limestone tomb was finished in 1858 at a cost of $7,000—about $200,000 in today's money—and Ira was laid to rest in it. That should have been the end of his story.

But by 1865, Chicago was having problems with its municipal cemetery. Some of the dead did not stay fully buried in the sandy ground near the lake. Besides, the city was growing up around the site. And unlike the situation in Boston, old burial grounds did not increase the value of nearby property. In 1869 Chicago City Cemetery was taken over by the Lincoln Park Commissioners for conversion to a park. The bodies were transferred to Graceland, Rosehill and other graveyards. The adjacent Catholic cemetery was also vacated, with that land used for a new archbishop's residence.

A lonely mausoleum in a onetime cemetery—the Couch Tomb in Lincoln Park. *Photo by the author.*

Transforming the cemetery into a park took more than twenty years. With the dawn of the twentieth century, all remnants of the graveyard were gone—all except Ira Couch's mausoleum. Why it remains there is debated by historians.

The usual explanation is that the Couch family fought removal of the tomb all the way to the U.S. Supreme Court and won its case. However, nobody has found any documentary evidence of such a decision. More likely, the mausoleum was left standing because neither the park commissioners nor the Couch family wanted to pay for tearing it down. That's the kind of explanation that makes sense in Chicago.

When I first started visiting Lincoln Park in the 1960s, the Couch Tomb was barely visible behind a massive growth of shrubbery. Officials were trying to hide it. They were worried that people might not want to go picnicking in a onetime graveyard.

After decades of neglect, the park district renovated the mausoleum in the 1990s. The shrubs were cut down, and the limestone structure itself was repaired. Now a spotlight illuminates it at night. The civic embarrassment has become a point of civic pride.

The next step will probably be to open the Couch Tomb to the public and charge admission.

Part III

HIDDEN LANDMARKS

SOUTH

Bet-a-Million

Michigan Avenue south of 26th Street was once called Millionaires' Row. In those days, at the turn of the twentieth century, $1 million was a real fortune, not merely the walking-around money of utility infielders or personal injury lawyers. The avenue was thick with mansions.

Time passed, the neighborhood declined and the mansions were carved up into rooming houses. Then came the bulldozers. Then came urban renewal. Drive down that stretch of Michigan today and you'll think you are in Schaumburg.

A few of the grand homesteads have survived. The most historic of them is located at 2944 South Michigan Avenue. Here was the home of John Warne Gates, better known as "Bet-a-Million" Gates. That was a helluva nickname to live up to, and Gates did. But before he could bet a million, he had to get much more.

Gates was born on a farm near what is now West Chicago in 1855. At twenty he went out on the road as a traveling salesman for a new invention, barbed wire. To showcase his product in Texas, Gates rented a plaza in San Antonio, strung it with the wire and invited skeptical cattlemen to put their wildest cattle inside. The cattle stayed put, and Gates was overwhelmed with orders for barbed wire—so many orders that the factory couldn't keep up with the demand.

So Gates opened his own barbed wire factory. He made money there and moved into the oil business. With even more money from oil, he became a major-league stock speculator. Wall Street insiders said that Gates was one of the few people clever enough to outmaneuver J.P. Morgan.

Back to the nickname. Many tales are told about how Gates earned it. He won $1 million betting on a single horse race in Britain. He won more than $1 million in an all-night poker game while traveling by train from Chicago to New York. He lost $1 million betting on which raindrop would get to the bottom of a window first. Any of the stories could be true—or none of them. Maybe it was simply the mystique that surrounded the man.

John Warne Gates, aka Bet-a-Million Gates. *Author's collection.*

The mansion on Michigan Avenue was built for Chicago financier Sydney Kent in 1883. The architecture was by the firm of Burnham & Root. It later used variations on the sculptured masonry style in the Rookery and Monadnock buildings downtown. Gates bought the mansion in 1897. That was one of his better years—he cleared $12 million on stock market manipulations alone. If you check out that number on an inflation calculator, it works out to nearly $400 million today.

Once he settled in, Gates solidified his reputation as a lavish party-giver. An invitation to one of his bashes was a social triumph. "The crystal chandeliers in the great paneled rooms often burned brightly far into the night," one journalist wrote. "The porte-cochere on the north side of the house was always a stir with the arrival or departure of polished carriages and coaches-and-four."

Gates lived in the Michigan Avenue mansion for less than ten years. He later moved his family to New York to be closer to the financial action. He died in 1911.

Back in Chicago, his onetime home passed through many stages. An Indianapolis millionaire named M.D. Spades bought it from Gates. Later it was a college dormitory. The Catholic Youth Organization owned the property for a while, using it as a residence for unemployed young men. After that it became a convent and, during the 1980s, was converted to apartments. Today, it's condos. Since 1987 the mansion at 2944 South Michigan Avenue has been an official Chicago landmark called the Sydney Kent House.

By my calculation, John W. Gates lived in this building for about 7 percent of its history. But without the Gates connection, nobody but architectural historians would be talking about the place, and that fact should count for something. Go east and you can find a bunch of very old houses boasting that—for one night in 1777—"George Washington Slept Here." So put John W. Gates on the landmark designation, along with Sydney Kent. Give Bet-a-Million his due. At least he lived in the house long enough to have the snow shoveled.

Joe Louis Home

Joe Louis was born in Alabama and grew up in Detroit. He spent his later life in Las Vegas. But during the twelve years he reigned as heavyweight boxing champion of the world, he lived in Chicago.

Born Joseph Louis Barrow in 1914, he dropped his last name when he began amateur boxing as a Detroit teenager so his mother wouldn't find out what he was doing. As Joe Louis, the kid fighter attracted the attention of John Roxborough. Roxborough was one of the city's gambling kingpins and became Louis's manager.

In 1934 Louis turned pro. Roxborough began grooming him for a shot at the heavyweight championship, and that meant a move to Chicago, where Louis could train under Jack Blackburn. Chicago promoter Julian Black joined Roxborough as a partner and found Louis an apartment on 46th Street off South Park Way (now King Drive).

Louis quickly rose through the ranks with a string of knockouts. During one of his gym sessions, he noticed Marva Trotter, a secretary at the *Chicago Daily Defender* newspaper. They started dating. On the morning of September 24, 1935, Joe and Marva were married in New York. Joe then went off to Yankee Stadium, knocked out ex-champ Max Baer in four rounds and went back to his hotel and Marva.

The new couple settled in at the Rosenwald Apartments at 4648 South Michigan Avenue. The 454-unit complex had been built by white philanthropist Julius Rosenwald to provide decent housing for the city's African Americans. Louis later said that the Rosenwald "was the most fabulous building black people could live in at the time." Gwendolyn Brooks, Nat King Cole and other prominent Chicagoans were also residents.

Louis continued winning in the ring until Max Schmeling stopped him in June 1936. Louis then rebounded with a new string of victories. On June 22, 1937, he knocked out James J. Braddock at Comiskey Park to become the new heavyweight champion.

Marva was not at the fight. According to the *Chicago Tribune*, she listened to the action on the radio in their home at 4320 South Michigan Avenue. After the fight, Louis had trouble driving the few blocks home through the crowds. "I thought all of Chicago was standing outside my house," he wrote in his autobiography. "Marva and I had to come out, I don't know how many times, and wave at the people."

Exactly when the Louises relocated from the Rosenwald is unclear. According to the 1940 census, Joe had purchased the three-story apartment building for $7,500—about $140,000 in today's money. Their personal flat had five rooms. At that time, the tenants in the other five units paid rents ranging from $40 to $65 a month.

Apartment building owned by Joe Louis during his reign as heavyweight boxing champ. *Photo by the author.*

One year to the day after he'd won the heavyweight title, Louis took care of his old nemesis, Max Schmeling, in just over two minutes. In the course of twelve years, Louis would successfully defend his title twenty-five times, more than any other boxing champion. Some critics scoffed at his challengers as the Bum-of-the-Month Club. More likely, Louis was just too good for anyone.

Louis served in the army during World War II, mostly fighting exhibitions. When he came out of the service, his skills had noticeably deteriorated. He won a few fights, but the magic was gone. In October 1949, he announced his retirement from the ring.

Meanwhile, Louis's marriage had also deteriorated. The ladies liked Joe, and Joe liked the ladies. Joe and Marva divorced in 1945, remarried in 1946 and then divorced a final time in 1949. Marva kept the two children and the apartment building on Michigan Avenue.

The rest of Louis's life was not happy. He had trusted too many people with his money, and the Internal Revenue Service came after him for back taxes, which he couldn't pay. A boxing comeback was an embarrassment. He had health problems and battled substance abuse. His final years were spent as a greeter in a casino.

Joe Louis died in 1981. He was buried at Arlington National Cemetery. A few years after his death, his favorite local golf course—Pipe O' Peace in Riverdale—was renamed Joe Louis the Champ Golf Course. The apartment building he owned on Michigan Avenue during his glory years remains a private residence.

THE O'LEARY HIMSELF

What would you do if your mother destroyed Chicago? That was the problem for James Patrick O'Leary. In 1871, when Little Jimmy was two years old, fire broke out in the barn behind the family home on De Koven Street. The flames spread, and within two days, most of Chicago had burned down. Somehow the legend grew that Mrs. Catherine O'Leary's cow had kicked over a lantern and started the whole disaster.

Well, what would you do if you were Little Jimmy O'Leary? You'd grow up into Big Jim O'Leary, the gambling king of the Stock Yards.

O'Leary started small time, running errands for local bookies. His major coup came in 1892. Heavyweight boxing champ John L. Sullivan was defending his title against James J. Corbett. The smart operators thought that nobody could beat the great John L., certainly not a fancy-dan like Corbett. O'Leary liked the challenger and bet everything he had on Corbett at odds of 4-to-1 or better. When Corbett won, Big Jim had his first stake.

He now opened what was euphemistically known as a "resort," at Halsted and 42nd Streets, across from the main entrance to the Yards. The license said that O'Leary was operating a saloon, and the property also included a bowling alley, billiard parlor and Turkish bath. But soon everybody in the city knew that you could get down a bet at Big Jim's place.

O'Leary prospered. He married and started a family—there would eventually be two sons and three daughters. In 1901 he built an elaborate thirty-three-room Renaissance chateau at 726 West Garfield Boulevard, a few doors down from the fashionable Chicago Bicycle Club. The architect was Zachary Taylor Davis, who later designed both the city's ballparks. There is no record that O'Leary kept a cow in a barn in the rear.

Long before suburban shopping malls, O'Leary started a branch location in Du Page County. Called the Stockade, it opened in 1904. Local officials were paid $5,000 a week to look the other way while the Santa Fe Railroad ran Gamblers' Special trains, and for a while, the place boomed. Then some reformer busybodies got into the act. Big Jim had to close the Stockade and pay a $1,700 fine.

Garfield Boulevard mansion built by gambler Big Jim O'Leary, son of *the* Mrs. O'Leary. *Photo by the author.*

There were other attempts to diversify. O'Leary operated a gambling ship on the lake called the *City of Traverse*, but had to junk the venture after three years—according to one story, he refused to bribe the shore-bound police on principle, so they raided the ship every time it docked. In 1907 he organized a syndicate and opened an amusement grove at Halsted and 51st Streets called Luna Park. That lasted four years. The original Stock Yards gambling resort remained Big Jim's main business.

Before every election, reporters would descend on O'Leary's resort to have the proprietor predict the outcome. With much ceremony, Big Jim would make his pronouncement. It was fine entertainment in the era before public opinion polls, and O'Leary called the winner often enough to keep his reputation as a seer intact.

He was a product of his times. Big Jim O'Leary stayed in business because the public felt that gambling was a personal vice that didn't harm society. The anti-gambling laws were not often enforced. Of course, it helped if you paid off the right people.

Eventually the city grew up. Prohibition came, and the feds took the letter of the law more seriously than Chicago officials did. Raiders found a cache of illegal whiskey in the basement of the Halsted Street resort. In court Big Jim produced a pharmacist license and claimed that he was selling the whiskey for medicinal purposes. The judge ordered him shut down anyway.

He was soon back in business, but it wasn't fun anymore. There were more raids. O'Leary talked about retiring. Maybe he'd write his memoirs. After all, he told his friends in the press, he was a millionaire several times over and didn't need the headaches.

Like any gambler, Big Jim O'Leary knew that you had to keep up a good front. When he died in 1925, his entire estate was valued at $10,200. His Halsted Street resort was torn down several years later. The mansion on Garfield Boulevard remains, privately owned.

THE SENATOR AND THE PINEAPPLE

During the first decades of the twentieth century, Charles S. Deneen was a major player in Chicago politics. He had come to the city from downstate in the 1880s to study law. Once he had passed the bar, he became involved in Republican politics. Deneen was elected to the Illinois House of Representatives in 1892. Four years later, he was elected Cook County state's attorney. And after two terms in that office, he was elected governor of Illinois in 1904.

Deneen served two terms as governor and then lost a bid for a third term in 1912. Yet he was hardly through with politics. He remained leader of the "good government" wing of the GOP. In 1924 he beat incumbent U.S. Senator Medill McCormick in the Republican primary and then went on to win the general election. During these years, he settled into a sumptuous three-story frame residence at 457 West 61st Place in Englewood, the South Side's dynamic "city within a city."

Deneen had allied himself with former Chicago mayor William Hale Thompson to bring down their common enemy, McCormick. But when Thompson ran for his old office in 1927, the senator refused to support him. Thompson won anyway. That set the stage for a showdown in the 1928 spring primaries.

The Thompson faction had close ties to various underworld figures. A civic leader who visited Al Capone's office noted that Capone had pictures of three statesmen on display: George Washington, Abraham Lincoln and Big Bill Thompson. Still, Senator Deneen was not afraid to get his hands dirty when politics demanded it. One of his staunchest allies was Diamond Joe Esposito, Nineteenth Ward Republican committeeman, restaurant owner and bootlegger.

Both Thompson and Deneen fielded rival slates in the April 10 Republican primary. The greatest local interest was in the contest for state's attorney. Thompson was backing incumbent Robert Crowe. Deneen supported the challenger, "honest judge" John A. Swanson. The campaign grew intense. Then the bombings started.

The homes of two prominent Thompson allies were hit with hand grenades. Deneen supporters had their homes attacked in retaliation. The contemporary slang term for a hand grenade was a "pineapple." So many grenades were going off that the newspapers began referring to the campaign as the "Pineapple Primary."

On March 21, unknown drive-by gunmen killed Diamond Joe Esposito, in front of his wife and daughter, near the family home on Oakley Boulevard. Senator Deneen was in Washington when he received the news. He immediately came back to Chicago. The senator attended Esposito's funeral on the morning of March 26 and then returned to Washington by train.

Shortly after 11:00 p.m. that evening, a bomb exploded on the porch of Deneen's Englewood home. The blast tore away the front of the house and smashed all the windows. The windows of a dozen nearby buildings were shattered as well.

Englewood home of U.S. Senator Charles Deneen, now abandoned. *Photo by the author.*

Awakened by the explosion, people rushed into the street. Police and emergency crews arrived. One of the neighbors said she had heard the blast and then saw a man jump into a car and speed away. Now reporters descended on the scene, and they brought chilling news: a few miles away on Crandon Avenue, the home of candidate Swanson had also been bombed.

No one was hurt in either incident. But the attack on Senator Deneen's residence made national headlines. It was one thing for those barbarians in Chicago to shoot one another, but you did not bomb the home of a United States senator. There were calls for an investigation by the U.S. attorney general and suggestions that President Coolidge should put the city under martial law. One newspaper columnist was inspired to present a local version of the national anthem:

> *The rocket's red glare,*
> *The bombs bursting in air,*
> *Gave proof to the world*
> *That Chicago's still there.*

The Thompson faction claimed that Deneen and Swanson had bombed their own homes to gain sympathy. Few people swallowed that one. In the April 10 primary, the entire Thompson-backed ticket lost.

Swanson beat Crowe and later won the general election for Cook County state's attorney.

Senator Charles Deneen ran for reelection in 1930 but lost in a violence-free primary. He died in 1940. The house on 61st Place has now been abandoned for several years, its fate uncertain.

AL CAPONE HOME

Nearly ninety years have passed since the federal government sent Al Capone into involuntary retirement. Many of the landmarks of his career are gone. Yet his family home still stands at 7244 South Prairie Avenue.

With his wife, Mae, and their infant son, Capone arrived in Chicago from Brooklyn in 1919. He was twenty years old and had been hired as an enforcer by mob boss Johnny Torrio. At first the Capones rented an apartment on Wabash Avenue near Torrio headquarters. Al's elder brother, Ralph, and his wife soon joined them there.

By 1923 Al had risen to second-in-command of Torrio's organization. He wanted a nice, quiet place for his wife and son. The red brick two-flat he settled on in the Grand Crossing neighborhood had been built in 1905 at a reported cost of $5,000. Capone bought the building for $5,500—about $80,000 in today's money. The property was reportedly registered in Mae Capone's name.

Capone had a soft spot for his relatives, and he wanted them near him. He brought his widowed mother, Teresa, to Chicago from Brooklyn, along with his two younger sisters. Again there was room for brother Ralph, who now had two children of his own.

The newly purchased building had fifteen rooms. Al took the seven rooms on the first floor for his wife, son, mother and sisters. Ralph's family occupied the eight rooms upstairs. In later years, two other Capone brothers also lived in the second-floor flat.

When the Capones moved into the two-flat, the most noteworthy thing about the family was that they were Italians settling in a mostly Irish area. Al was not yet a celebrity. He told neighbors he was a secondhand furniture dealer. He enrolled his youngest sister in a private girls' school nearby, where he delighted in playing Santa Claus at Christmas.

Al personalized his residence with some special touches. For the master bath, he imported a seven-foot tub from Germany. The basement walls were reinforced with concrete a foot thick, to make them resistant to bullets. Steel doors were installed on the outside of the house, and steel bars were set in the

Two-flat home of Al Capone and assorted family members. *Photo by the author.*

ground-floor windows. An oversize brick garage was built to accommodate Al's big armored cars.

While the Capones were getting settled on Prairie Avenue, Chicago mayor William E. Dever was cracking down on the illegal liquor trade. The Torrio outfit moved its operations to suburban Cicero. Although Al began spending many nights at the Hawthorne Hotel there, he kept his family in the Prairie Avenue two-flat.

Chicagoans first became acquainted with the Capone residence in 1924, when his brother Frank was waked there after being killed in a police shootout. As Al became more famous, his home was often in the news. Visiting reporters knew that he was good copy, and they sometimes got a plate of home-cooked spaghetti during an interview. By the time Dever and his cleanup were voted out in 1927, Capone had become the new mob boss.

Back from his Cicero exile, Al established headquarters in the Lexington Hotel, just south of the Loop. As his business expanded, he spent even less time on Prairie Avenue. In 1929 he moved to Florida. He maintained his official residence in that state, through all his legal setbacks, until his death in 1947.

Meanwhile, Al's mother and various Capone siblings continued living on Prairie Avenue. Teresa died in 1952, and the family sold the building. Since then it has passed through several owners.

In 1989 the Capone home was nominated for placement in the National Register of Historic Places. Jesse James's last home in St. Joseph, Missouri, had already been added to the list and had even been converted into a museum. "[Capone] was a historical fact," one historian said in defending the idea. "He lived here, and we need to come to terms with that." However, Italian American organizations, city and state agencies and other concerned citizens immediately launched a protest, and the proposal was withdrawn.

A few years ago there were reports that the current owner was putting the property up for sale. Preservationists were concerned that a purchaser might tear down the building. At this writing the two-flat at 7244 South Prairie Avenue has survived, a private residence.

MAHALIA JACKSON HOME

Mahalia Jackson was one of the thousands of black southerners moving north to Chicago during the first decades of the twentieth century. She arrived in the city in 1927, when she was sixteen. As a young woman she opened both a beauty salon and a flower shop. But Jackson's real talent was in singing. Over the course of forty years she became the most celebrated gospel singer in the world.

The Chicago Tribune marker in front of her onetime home at 8358 South Indiana Avenue tells us as much about Mahalia Jackson. What it doesn't tell us about is the struggles she had merely to live there.

Jackson liked to practice her singing while she cooked and cleaned her flat at night. The landlord complained about the noise, so Jackson saved her money and bought her own apartment building. That didn't work either—now her tenants were saying she was too loud.

So, in 1956, Jackson decided that the only solution was to buy a house for herself. Driving around the Chatham neighborhood on the South Side, she stopped at a number of homes with "For Sale" signs out front. At each one, she was told that the property had just been sold. Chatham was an all-white area. Although restrictive covenants had been outlawed by the U.S. Supreme Court, that didn't seem to matter. "The attention I had been getting from white people for my singing had sort of confused me," Jackson wrote later. "They still didn't want me as their neighbor."

Jackson then went to a real estate agent. A white surgeon had a house on the market on the northwest corner of Indiana Avenue and 84th Street. Told the identity of the prospective buyer, the surgeon said he was "proud to sell my house to [Mahalia Jackson]." The final price was $40,000—about $370,000 in today's money.

Mahalia Jackson's house, where she could finally practice her singing. *Photo by the author.*

The news of Jackson's purchase sent the neighborhood into frenzy. A local Catholic priest who tried to calm things was ignored. Protest meetings were held. Jackson received hostile phone calls at all hours of the night, threatening to dynamite the house.

The situation didn't improve when she moved in. Rifle bullets were fired through her window. A police guard was posted and remained in front of the house for nearly a year. "I hadn't intended to start a crusade," Jackson recalled. "All I wanted was a quiet, pretty home to live in."

When it became clear that Jackson wasn't going to be driven out, the overt violence subsided. Meanwhile, she bought new furniture and began making improvements on the property. She built an addition on the rear of the house, with a veranda enclosed by a wrought-iron fence. It reminded her of the French Quarter homes in her native New Orleans.

Early in 1958 Edward R. Murrow brought his *Person-to-Person* television program to Indiana Avenue. The show's format called for Murrow to interview the singer in her home. Jackson used the occasion to invite the local kids over for ice cream and cake, as well as a chance to appear on TV. Many of the children did show up, convincing Jackson that she was finally being accepted.

A cynic once described integration as "the time between the first black family moving in, and the last white family moving out." That was the case in Jackson's neighborhood. Scared by panic-peddling realtors and afflicted by their own prejudice, all the whites eventually left.

Jackson remained in her Chatham home until moving to Hyde Park in 1970. She did not immediately sell the Indiana Avenue property, and the house remained vacant for two years. Shortly before her death in 1972, she sold the property to a young banker named Roland Burris. Burris later entered politics, eventually becoming a United States senator. At this writing, he continues to live in the house, still a private residence.

"The white people swore we would ruin it," Jackson wrote about the Chatham neighborhood in her 1966 autobiography. "They said it would be a slum overnight. But it hasn't changed. The grass is still green. The lawns are as neat as ever. Children still whiz up and down on their bikes."

So it was in 1966. And so it remains today.

CHICAGO'S OLDEST PUBLIC MONUMENT

Chicago has hundreds of statues, monuments and historical markers. But unless you do a little exploring, you are likely to miss the oldest one: the Illinois-Indiana State Line Boundary Marker.

Indiana became a state in 1816, Illinois two years later. Originally, the northern border of each state was supposed to be a line drawn through the southern tip of Lake Michigan. But for various reasons, Congress allowed Indiana's border with the Michigan Territory to be shifted ten miles northward. The Illinois border with the Wisconsin Territory was also moved north, a full fifty-one miles from that southern tip of the lake.

Meanwhile, the boundary line between the two new states had to be precisely determined. In 1818 Illinois and Indiana hired two surveyors to map out their common border. The work was completed three years later, and both states agreed with the measurement. A pine post was set up to mark the northern endpoint of the line, along the Lake Michigan shore.

Then, in 1833, Congress ordered a new survey of the Illinois-Indiana border. The second survey was completed the following year and didn't change anything. However, the United States surveyor general was then ordered to replace the pine post with a more permanent boundary marker—something that would be "as economical as it is practical."

In the fall of 1838 the improved marker was set in place on the lakeshore, straddling the state line. Built of sandstone, it was an angled obelisk, fifteen feet high. The name of the marker's designer is lost to history. Nor is there any surviving documentation on the cost of its construction or on how the government contract was obtained.

The boundary marker site was isolated in 1838. When the winds blew across the sandy beach, the shifting dunes often covered it completely. The newly incorporated city of Chicago was more than ten miles away.

Over the next century, civilization grew out to meet the marker. The shoreline was extended north by landfill. Then multiple railroad lines came through the area. The South Park commissioners laid out Calumet Park. In 1929 Commonwealth Edison built a huge electrical generating plant nearby.

By the 1980s the state line marker had become neglected and vandalized among the rail yards. Allen J. Benson, a ComEd executive, convinced the company to sponsor its restoration in conjunction with the East Side Historical Society and other interested groups. In 1988 the marker was moved 190 feet north to its present location, just outside the plant gate. A new base was added at that time. Before the work was finished, Benson died. A plaque next to the boundary marker was dedicated to his memory.

Chicago's oldest public monument—and Hammond's too, for that matter—is difficult to find. The obelisk is located at what would be the intersection of State Line Road and 103rd Street. The best way to get there is to approach from the north, via 95th Street.

Go east on 95th Street past Ewing Avenue and then turn right onto Crilly Drive. Continue south on Crilly Drive, along the western edge of Calumet

Illinois-Indiana Boundary Marker of 1838, Chicago's oldest public monument. *Photo by the author.*

Park, to the junction with Avenue G. Turn right on Avenue G and keep going south past the park's field house, until you arrive at 100th Street. Now you will see some grade-level railroad tracks on your right. Just before the tracks and parallel to them, a small access road continues south-southeast. Follow this road to its end, the site of the old ComEd plant and the boundary marker.

The access road you just took doesn't have an official name. This has led to some confusion. Since the road continues the general route of Avenue G, many reference sources will tell you that the Illinois-Indiana State Line Boundary Marker is located on Avenue G, at 103rd Street-extended. There's a problem with that—a few blocks away, there is a real intersection of Avenue G and 103rd Street.

The solution to this mess is simple: name the access road along the tracks "Allen J. Benson Drive." It would be an appropriate way to remember a public-spirited businessman who had a sense of history. And how expensive are a few street signs?

THE REAL "CHRISTMAS STORY" HOUSE

One of the delights of the holiday season is the annual rebroadcast of *A Christmas Story*. If you've somehow missed this movie, it is a tale set in a fictitious midwestern city, in an unspecified year around 1940, centering on the everyday adventures of nine-year-old Ralphie Parker. The hook is Ralphie's ongoing yearning for a particular Christmas present, namely an Official Red Ryder Carbine Action Two-Hundred Shot Range Model Air Rifle.

Radio raconteur Jean Shepherd's short stories are the inspiration for the movie. Before filming began in 1983, Shepherd scouted locations that reminded him of his boyhood in Hammond and settled on a cottage in the Tremont section of Cleveland. In 2005 that house at 3159 West Eleventh Street was purchased by an enterprising entrepreneur who converted it into the Christmas Story House Museum. Across the street is a gift shop that sells such artifacts as bunny playsuits and electric-sex leg lamps.

But if you are looking for a closer connection to the real events behind the story, you can join the fans who make a drive-by pilgrimage past Shepherd's actual boyhood home. The frame bungalow is located at 2907 Cleveland Street, just off Kennedy Avenue in Hammond.

Jean Parker Shepherd Jr. was born on Chicago's South Side in 1921—about ten years before Ralphie Parker—the son of a dairy clerk. Along with his younger brother, Randall, he grew up in Hammond and attended Warren G.

Harding Elementary School. Jean graduated from Hammond High School in 1939. During World War II he served stateside in the army.

After the war Shepherd began his career as a radio broadcaster in Hammond. He moved up through several larger markets, finally landing in New York in 1955. All the while he was establishing himself as a storyteller, gentle yet biting. Before there was Garrison Keillor, there was Jean Shepherd.

Shepherd also began writing short stories for magazines. The first collection of his tales, titled *In God We Trust: All Others Pay Cash*, appeared in 1966. Many of the incidents in the movie are drawn from this book. At various times he hosted different idiosyncratic series on public TV, most memorably *Jean Shepherd's America*. By 1980 he had a nationwide cult following.

Yet it was the 1983 release of *A Christmas Story* that introduced Shepherd to the greater population. Although he continued to churn out stories and do the occasional radio or TV gig, the movie's popularity fixed his reputation. When he died in 1999, the lede of his obituaries usually referred to him as the "author and narrator of the beloved holiday film."

The Shepherd family lived in various places around Hammond during the 1930s. They moved into the house at 2907 Cleveland Street in 1935. The 1,032-square-foot bungalow dates from the early twentieth century. A carving in the attic contains the autographs "17 yrs. old. Jean Shepherd. 2/18/39" and "15 yrs. old. Randall Shepherd. 2/28/39."

The Hammond home where Jean Shepherd lived out "A Christmas Story." *Photo by the author.*

Unlike the museum in Cleveland, the Cleveland Street house in Hammond is a private residence and does not welcome visitors. When the movie came out, the current occupants knew nothing about its pedigree. Then one day, Randall Shepherd arrived in a limousine and asked to look around. The lady of the house turned him down because "she didn't know him from Adam." It was not until years later that the residents discovered the graffiti in the attic.

The Shepherd boys' alma mater, Warren G. Harding Elementary School, still educates young Hammondonians at 3211 165th Street, a few blocks east of their onetime home. Their cinema counterparts, Ralphie and Randy, had a much longer commute. The school used in the movie is in Saint Catherines, Ontario, more than two hundred miles from the Christmas Story House in Cleveland.

Shepherd's stories are set in the Indiana town of "Hohman," an obvious reference to one of Hammond's main streets. During his lifetime, he did not foster a close relationship with his hometown. However, in more recent years, the City of Hammond has recognized its most famous son with the Jean Shepherd Community Center in Dowling Park and an annual Jean Shepherd Holiday Kickoff Festival in November.

THE ENCHANTED LAKE

They say that somewhere on the far South Side of Chicago there was once a large lake. It sprawled over the map, bigger than the grand West Side parks. Old newspaper stories talked about it. Grandparents told their grandkids about picnics on its shore or fishing in its waters. But in our time, like an enchanted memory, the lake has disappeared.

Well, not quite. Drive out on the Bishop Ford Freeway past 115th Street. If you look carefully to the east, you can still find bits of Lake Calumet.

The southeast corner of Chicago is marshland. Nineteenth-century maps show three miniature lakes here, remnants of the retreating glacier, clustered around the Indiana border. They were Hyde Lake, Wolf Lake and Lake George. To the west of this trio was big brother Lake Calumet.

Calumet is an English corruption from a native word meaning "peace pipe." Historians believe that local tribes had a settlement nearby. When George Pullman built his company town to the west in the 1880s, residents used Lake Calumet to unwind. The lake was roughly oval-shaped, stretching from 103rd to 130th Street.

The area was then being transformed by industrial development. In the 1909 *Plan of Chicago*, Daniel Burnham foresaw a mixed-use future for the lake. "The country is gently undulating, with plenty of woodland, and the view across Lake Calumet is fine," he wrote. Burnham thought that the area around the lake itself should be reserved as parkland.

However, the future of Lake Calumet went in another direction. During the 1920s, the City of Chicago decided to turn the lake into a harbor. Work began filling in the northern part. This was considered progress. As one alderman put it, the lake itself was "nothing more than a breeding place for mosquitoes and mud turtles."

In the decades that followed, the lake was transformed. The landfill was expanded, becoming a convenient—and sometimes illegal— dumping ground. Burnham's proposed parkway around the perimeter became a six-lane expressway down the western shore. The opening of the St. Lawrence Seaway in 1959 promised to make Chicago an international port, and the harbor facilities were expanded to meet future traffic. By now Lake Calumet had been reduced to about a third of its original size.

Politicians still tinkered with plans for the area. During the 1980s there were proposals for a 1992 Chicago world's fair, to celebrate the 500th anniversary of Columbus's voyage and the almost-centennial of the Columbian Exposition. One of the sites suggested was the property around Lake Calumet. The fair never went past the talking stage.

In the 1990s discussion began about a third Chicagoland airport. Expansion of the existing Gary airport was one possibility; building a new facility in Peotone was another. Then Chicago mayor Richard M. Daley came up with his own plan for a site just east of Lake Calumet that would ensure that airport revenues went into the city coffers. That idea never became reality either.

Today, more than a century of dumping has taken its toll on the lake and its surroundings. The Environmental Protection Agency launched a cleanup in 2010. The Lake Calumet Cluster was put on the agency's National Priorities List as one of the nation's worst hazardous waste sites.

Meanwhile, the St. Lawrence Seaway has never produced the expected shipping traffic. The Illinois International Port District (IIPD) has facilities on Lake Calumet, as well as in other places. Some years ago, the IIPD opened the Harborside International Golf Center on lake landfill. The center features two upscale courses, with views of the faraway Loop and nearby auto graveyard.

Visitors to what is left of Lake Calumet will find its perimeter fenced. Considering the waste hazards, that's probably a good thing. On Earth Day, the IIPD has allowed a local environmental group to give walking tours of the properties.

What to do with Lake Calumet remains a topic of debate. The IIPD continues to operate. Activists continue to lobby for more public access and implementation of Daniel Burnham's century-old vision. For now, be assured that the lake is still there east of the Bishop Ford. And take a moment to look skyward. Sometimes you can spot a bald eagle.

CHICAGO'S SMALLEST CEMETERY

The smallest cemetery in the city of Chicago measures little more than one hundred square feet and is located on the Southeast Side, in the middle of a scrapyard off Ewing Avenue. It has one permanent resident, Andreas von Zirngibl.

Zirngibl was born in 1797. His birthplace is given as either Bavaria or Russia, and his early life and the extent of his schooling are also undetermined. At eighteen he was a soldier in the Prussian army. He fought at Waterloo and helped beat Napoleon, although he came out of the battle with only one arm.

Settling in Bavaria after the war, Zirngibl worked as a fisherman along the Danube River—in the nineteenth century, a challenging occupation for someone with only one arm. In any event, Andreas persisted. He married and began raising a family.

Around 1850 Zirngibl, his wife and their five children came to America. Revolutionary upheavals were rocking Germany, and the family was one among thousands abandoning their homeland. At first they lived near Milwaukee. Andreas fished in Lake Michigan.

Then, in 1854, the Zirngibls moved down the lake past Chicago, establishing their household near the Indiana border. Andreas went on fishing. Finding a good spot in the lake and wanting a convenient base nearby, he bought a forty-acre parcel of marshy land near the mouth of the Calumet River for $160 in gold. He promptly set up a shack on the property.

Less than a year after buying the land at the river mouth, Andreas caught a fever. He died on August 21, 1855. According to his family, the old fisherman's last wish was to be buried near his favorite fishing grounds. He was laid to rest on the Calumet River property beneath a wooden cross, the grave site enclosed by a white picket fence. Although the Zirngibl family later dispersed, they continued to make regular visits to tend the grave.

Meanwhile, urban growth spread to the mouth of the Calumet. By the early 1880s, the property was in the hands of the Calumet & Chicago Canal and Dock Company. Now the Zirngibl family brought suit to reclaim the land where Andreas was buried.

The case had one major complication: the Great Fire of 1871 had destroyed many of the city's property records. The Zirngibl family said that their deed must have been lost in the fire. The canal company contended that Andreas had been a squatter and had never actually purchased the property and that the family had no legal title to the land.

In 1895 the Illinois Supreme Court heard arguments in the suit. The Zirngibl case suffered a setback with the discovery that other bodies had been buried on the land. One witness claimed that Andreas had actually died in Whiting and had no connection with the Calumet River property before he was laid to rest there. The court finally decided that the canal company owned the land.

In explaining the decision, Justice David J. Baker noted that the Zirngibls had never made a claim on the property until it became valuable. At the same time, the court recognized the family's devotion in caring for the grave over the course of decades. So, in a ruling worthy of Solomon, the court decreed that Andreas should remain where he was and that his family be given free access to visit him.

Guarded by cement blocks, Chicago's one-man cemetery in a scrapyard. *Photo by the author.*

The years have passed. Various industrial operations have come and gone on the property near the river mouth. Every so often, the story of the cemetery in the scrapyard attracts the attention of the media. Even Mike Royko wrote about it.

In 1987 the Southeast Historical Society and the Zirngibl family raised money to restore the grave site. The white picket fence had not been sturdy enough to resist careless workers going about their everyday labor. Today, Andreas rests under a concrete slab surrounded by seven large concrete blocks. A granite headstone identifies him, although it has the wrong year for the Battle of Waterloo.

Chicago's one-man cemetery is located off East 93rd Court, at approximately 9331 South Ewing Avenue. Since this is private property and an active scrapyard, access is limited—unless you are a descendant of Andreas von Zirngibl.

THE RICHEST BLACK MAN IN AMERICA

Today, the street where Jesse Binga lived is named for Dr. Martin Luther King Jr. That's appropriate. When the street was called South Park Avenue and Binga lived at no. 5922, the house became a symbol of the civil rights struggle.

Jesse Binga was a self-starter. Born in Detroit in 1865, he first worked as a barber like his father. Dropping out of high school, he moved through a number of jobs in the western states before settling in Chicago at the time of the 1893 world's fair. A few years later, he entered the real estate business.

Although Chicago's African American population had always been small, that was changing as the twentieth century got underway. Southern blacks were moving north. At first, the newcomers settled in the city's traditional black district, a few blocks on either side of State Street on the Near South Side. As more settlers arrived, they began to burst the boundaries of the so-called Black Belt.

Here Binga saw his opportunity. Panicky whites in adjoining blocks were eager to sell. Binga was usually able to buy a property at rock-bottom price and then fix it up. Sometimes he divided a large living space into smaller units. He kept his costs low by doing most of the work himself. When all was done, he'd sell the property to a black buyer at a handsome profit. Jesse Binga became Chicago's leading agent of racial succession. He helped his people. And he got rich.

From real estate, Binga moved into banking. In 1908 he took over a failed bank at 3601 South State Street, reopening it as the Binga Bank. It was the city's first black-owned financial institution, and Binga promoted it heavily. Large display ads in the *Broad-ax* newspaper announced that the Binga Bank was paying 3 percent annual interest on savings accounts. Safe deposit boxes were also available for an annual rental of three dollars.

Now Binga's real estate business was reorganized as a department of the bank. He continued to handle all aspects of buying or selling property. As an added service, the bank began managing apartment houses for nonresident owners.

As his stature in the community grew, Binga became active in politics. Two years after opening his bank, he ran for a seat on the Cook County Board of Commissioners as a Republican, the party of choice for most African Americans at the time. Binga lost and made no further campaigns for elective office.

He moved to the South Park Avenue home in 1917. The Washington Park neighborhood was then all-white. Binga received death threats, and

BINGA STATE BANK
STATE STREET AND 35TH PLACE

We Work With You At All Times

THE BINGA STATE BANK is prepared to offer banking facilities to banks, corporations, churches, societies and individuals who have liquid assets and desire to raise quickly additional working capital for the promotion of their business.

THE RISING TIDE OF INDEPENDENCE ENGULFS THE SOUTH SIDE

A recent survey conducted by the South Side Property Owners' Association in Chicago, located south of Twenty-second Street, proved that 4,287 people of our group own one or more pieces of real estate, each ranging in price from $800.00 to $300,000.00. THE BINGA STATE BANK invites you to join its increasing number of depositors where loans may be negotiated — thus enhancing the value of your real estate.

Capital and Surplus	$120,000.00
Assets	681,448.33
Increase since June 30, 1922	164,169.35

The rapid increase in our assets is due to the implicit confidence the public has in the management of a conservative banking institution of our community.

MAKE IT YOUR BANK

BINGA STATE BANK
Under State Supervision and Member of Chicago Clearing House Association

One of a series of newspaper ads for Jesse Binga's bank. *From the Chicago Defender, October 21, 1922.*

the house was repeatedly bombed. When the police were slow to respond, he hired private twenty-four-hour security guards. Friends urged him to move. Binga defiantly refused. "I am an American citizen, a Christian, and a property owner," he told the *Chicago Defender*. "No man can make me a traitor or a coward. No power on earth can change my faith in God. I will defend my home and personal liberty to the extent of my life. I have just as much right to my home at Washington Park as anyone else." Years passed before the violence finally stopped.

The Binga business empire reached its peak during the 1920s. He rechartered the bank as the Binga State Bank and moved it into a newly built complex at the northwest corner of State and 35th Streets. Adjoining the bank was the five-story Binga Arcade, with stores, professional offices and a dance hall. Binga was spoken of as the richest black man in Chicago—or even in the entire United States.

His plans to open a federally chartered bank were stalled by the 1929 stock market crash. The Great Depression followed, and the Binga State Bank failed. Thousands of African American depositors were wiped out. Binga was wiped out, too. He served a prison term for embezzlement, although many people thought the charges were trumped up. The onetime multimillionaire spent his last years working as a janitor at St. Anselm Church, a few blocks from his home, for fifteen dollars per week.

Jesse Binga died in 1950. His onetime residence is a registered Chicago Landmark and is privately owned.

MARXISM ON THE GRAND BOULEVARD

The Grand Boulevard neighborhood has been the heart of Chicago's African American community since the 1920s. Before that, the area was German Jewish. From 1912 through 1920, the graystone three-flat at what is now 4512 South King Drive was home to Sam and Minnie Marx and their sons Julius, Adolph, Leonard, Milton and Herbert. The sons are better known by their stage names: Groucho, Harpo, Chico, Gummo and Zeppo.

The Marxes were originally New Yorkers. Sam was an easygoing tailor. Minnie had the brains and brass of the family. A performer herself, she raised her sons for careers in show business. During the first years of the new century, when the older boys were teens, they started singing in vaudeville. Minnie became their manager.

Various reasons are given for why the Marx family moved to Chicago. One story claims that a New York theatrical booker told Minnie that the boys would never make it in the big time, so she decided to try the Second City. Another source says that Minnie's brother Al Shean, a successful vaudeville comic, was living in Chicago and offered to help his nephews. Still, the most likely explanation was simple logistics. Chicago was the nation's rail hub. Travel on the vaudeville circuit would be easier from a central location. So, in 1910, the family moved.

Their first Chicago residence was in a walk-up apartment building at 4649 South Calumet Avenue. Two years later, Minnie scraped together a $1,000 down payment for the graystone on the boulevard. The purchase price was $25,000—about $650,000 in today's money.

The mortgage was held by their next-door neighbor, a man named Greenbaum. He became the family bogeyman. Whenever the brothers complained about their hectic life on the road, all Minnie would have to

Apartment building where the Marx Brothers spent most of their Chicago years. *Photo by the author.*

do is say the magic word, "Greenbaum." Then they'd shut up and get back to business.

By now the eldest brothers were young men. Their act gradually evolved into less singing and more comedy. During these years, when they collected their mail in Chicago, the Marx Brothers developed their familiar stage persona. They spent much of their summer downtime at nearby Comiskey Park, particularly when Ty Cobb and the Detroit Tigers came to town.

In 1917, just when the act was becoming successful, the United States entered World War I. The brothers weren't enthusiastic about getting drafted. But Minnie had read that farmers were exempt from military service, so she bought a farm. At least, that's the way the story is usually told. Once again, other sources tell a different tale—that the brothers were drafted but rejected on medical grounds.

The very urban Marxes now settled in on a farm in still-rural Countryside, northeast of the intersection of La Grange and Joliet Roads. They raised chickens, rabbits and guinea pigs. Or rather, they tried to raise them. Groucho said that whenever friends were coming out to visit, he had to go into LaGrange to buy eggs to put under their chickens so it would look like the farm was running smoothly.

Farmer or not, Gummo was drafted anyway. He hadn't been much of a performer and didn't like being on stage, so it was no great loss to the act. In later years he became an agent.

Minnie sold the Grand Boulevard home in 1920. The four Marx Brothers wanted to develop their act for the Broadway stage, and a move back to New York was in order. When their Broadway shows were successful, movies followed. As far as can be determined, none of them ever returned to visit their old South Side homestead. But when the brothers were invited to put their handprints in the sidewalk in front of Grauman's Chinese Theatre in Hollywood, Grouch quipped, "We know all about cement—we used to live in Chicago."

During the 1980s, when the city began surveying its historic buildings, the Marx Brothers home was missed. A 2003 *Chicago Tribune* story uncovered the oversight. Shortly afterward, an official Chicago Tribute "Marker of Distinction" was erected on the front parkway.

The graystone at 4512 South King Drive is a private residence. It is not known whether the current owner is named Greenbaum.

A FORGOTTEN HOME OF CLARENCE DARROW

Clarence Darrow is the most renowned trial lawyer in the annals of America. For the last thirty years of his life, he lived on the top floor of an apartment hotel facing Jackson Park. That building has been demolished. But a few miles to the north, at 4219 South Vincennes Avenue, a house that Darrow built still stands.

Darrow came to Chicago in an unlikely way. In 1887 he was thirty years old, married with a young son and a successful attorney in Ashtabula, Ohio. He put a down payment on a house. But at the last minute the seller backed out of the deal because of fear that Darrow could not make the payments. Darrow already had a brother and sister living in Chicago, so he decided to move there.

He opened a small practice and began making friends. In Ohio Darrow had been active in Democratic Party politics. About a year after arriving in Chicago, he landed a job as a city hall lawyer. Mayor DeWitt Cregier had heard Darrow speak at a political meeting and was impressed.

Cregier lost his reelection bid in 1891, so Darrow returned to the private sector. Besides his practice, he was hired as a counsel in the legal department of the Chicago & North Western Railroad. Much of his work involved defending the company against lawsuits brought by people who'd been injured at grade crossings.

Darrow's wife, Jessie, wanted a "normal bourgeois domestic life" for the couple and their son, Paul. At first Clarence obliged. Shortly after going to work for C&NW, he built the two-story graystone home on Vincennes Avenue in the fashionable Grand Boulevard neighborhood.

Darrow was ambitious. He had no false modesty about his own skills and no hesitancy about demanding top dollar for his services. Yet he had always had a gut feeling for society's underdogs. Now he was working for the fat cats. As one writer put it, he couldn't look himself in the mirror. He quit the railroad. Over the next five years, he began to become the Clarence Darrow of legend.

He represented labor leader Eugene V. Debs in court in the aftermath of the Pullman Strike, a case that gave him a national profile. He took his first murder case, defending the man who'd killed Mayor Carter Harrison. Darrow also found time to run an unsuccessful race for Congress on the Populist Party ticket in 1896. (Ironically, the party's presidential candidate that year was William Jennings Bryan, Darrow's opponent in the celebrated Scopes Monkey Trial three decades later.)

Clarence Darrow's forgotten home on Vincennes Avenue. *Photo by the author.*

He was spending less and less time on Vincennes Avenue. Jessie rarely saw him, except when he came home to sleep. By now Darrow's father was living in Chicago, and Clarence sometimes found it more convenient to bunk at his place. And Clarence was also meeting confident, sophisticated women who shared more of his developing interests. His marriage deteriorated.

Early in 1897 Darrow sued his wife for divorce on grounds of desertion. That was a convenient lie—Jessie had not deserted Clarence, he had deserted her. But divorce was still considered shameful. Because Jessie didn't want to hurt her husband's professional or political future, she agreed to go along with the charade.

The divorce was amicable. Jessie got the Vincennes Avenue house and $150 a month for the rest of her life. Clarence got his freedom. He later remarried and became famous, while his first wife and his son slipped into obscurity.

Clarence Darrow died in his apartment on East 60th Street on March 13, 1938. His ashes were scattered in a Jackson Park lagoon, and each year since then, admirers have held a memorial service at the site on the anniversary of his passing. About thirty years ago, reports began circulating that a ghostly figure resembling the great lawyer had been spotted wandering through the park. Since Darrow was a well-known skeptic of the supernatural, the identity of the apparition is open to question.

Meanwhile, there is the house on Vincennes Avenue. At the time of Darrow's death, the neighborhood around it was in decline. Somehow, despite a lack of official recognition, the building survived into the twenty-first century. A private residence, it has recently been renovated.

DALEY FAMILY HOME

The brick bungalow at 3536 South Lowe Avenue is the onetime home of two Chicago mayors, father and son. Since the Carter Harrison home on Ashland Boulevard was torn down many years ago, we must be talking about the Daleys.

The story begins half a block south, at 3602 South Lowe Avenue. In 1902 Richard Joseph Daley was born there, the son of an Irish sheet metal worker. He was an only child, a rarity in a neighborhood of large working-class families. After graduating from high school, Dick Daley went to work in the Stock Yards while studying law at DePaul at night. He also became a Democratic precinct captain.

Daley won his first election, to the Illinois House of Representatives, in 1936. Two years later, he moved up to the Illinois Senate. Meanwhile, he had married his longtime sweetheart, Eleanor Guilfoyle, forever known as "Sis."

In 1939 Daley built the house at 3536 South Lowe Avenue. The red brick bungalow is no different from hundreds of others scattered throughout the city, but it's clearly the best house on this block. Besides the senator, Sis and their two young daughters, Daley's parents moved in as well.

By that time, a number of Lithuanian families had joined the established Irish residents on Lowe Avenue. The 1940 census tells us that the block was home to various skilled and unskilled workers, two teachers and one state senator. Daley's $5,000-plus income was more than double that of any of the neighbors. He was doing so well that his father was able to retire in his mid-fifties.

Daley remained in the state Senate through 1946, when he ran for sheriff and lost. But in 1950 he became Cook County Clerk, and three years later, he was elected chairman of the county Democratic Party. In 1955 he used his position as party chairman to win election as mayor of Chicago.

All this time, Daley remained on Lowe Avenue—even when he no longer had to live in a senate district, even as his family grew to include seven children. Earlier Irish mayors and political bosses had moved to the city's finer neighborhoods once they could. New York City provided its mayor with swank Gracie Mansion. So, when Daley became mayor, well-meaning suggestions were floated that the Second City should have an official residence for its own chief executive.

A 1971 campaign booklet for Mayor Richard J. Daley. *Author's collection.*

Daley squelched the plan. He liked his home. And living on an everyday street among everyday people fit his image as an everyday guy who happened to be mayor. His decision to stay on Lowe Avenue was sincere but also politically astute—as was his everyday Chicago syntax and accent, which he reportedly could ditch when making a presentation to the municipal bond raters in New York.

Daley went on to be elected mayor six times. During those years, the house on Lowe Avenue was under twenty-four-hour guard by two Chicago police squad cars, one in front and one in the alley. The mayor kept his home private. Reporters were not welcome, and most longtime political associates never saw the inside of the house.

Richard J. Daley died in office of a heart attack in 1976. Twenty-five thousand people passed by his coffin at the all-night wake at Nativity of Our Lady Church, two blocks from his home. In the years afterward, the police detail remained in place for Sis Daley, a courtesy that had been extended to the widows of previous Chicago mayors.

Richard Michael Daley, the mayor's eldest son, was a thirty-four-year-old state senator in 1976, living in the old neighborhood not far from the house where he'd grown up. He had already followed his father into one political office. Now the politicos began speculating when the younger Daley would claim his inheritance as mayor of Chicago.

It did not come easily or overnight. Rich Daley was elected Cook County state's attorney in 1980 but lost his first bid for the mayoralty to Harold Washington in the 1983 Democratic primary. Then, in 1989, he was elected mayor in the special election after Washington's death. Daley II eventually surpassed his father's tenure in office, serving twenty-two years before retiring in 2011.

The Daley family home on Lowe Avenue remains a private residence.

Part IV

LOST LANDMARKS

Ronald Reagan's Chicago Home

The barricades went up in the fall of 2008. The Secret Service was securing the 5000 block of South Greenwood Avenue. Senator Barack Obama lived on that street. Now he had been elected president of the United States.

Obama was the first person to attain the country's highest office while a Chicago resident. But he was not the first president who'd ever lived in the city. A mile away and ninety-odd years before, the apartment building on the northeast corner of 57th Street and Maryland Avenue had been home to a future president named Ronald Reagan.

The Reagan family moved into a first-floor flat at 832 East 57th Street in January 1915. They had come to Chicago from the western Illinois village of Tampico. Jack Reagan, then in his early thirties, got a job selling shoes in the Loop. His wife, Nelle, stayed home with their two boys, six-year-old Neil and little Ron—called "Dutch"—who was going on four.

The University of Chicago was a few blocks east, but the area where the Reagans settled wasn't fashionable—nor was the apartment they rented. The cold-water flat was lighted by a single gas lamp, which operated when a quarter was deposited in a timer. Jack Reagan probably picked the location for its easy access to the Cottage Grove streetcar line.

After living in tiny Tampico, Chicago was a brave new world for little Dutch Reagan. He was excited to see all the people and activity. When a horse-drawn fire engine clanged by his bedroom window, he decided there could be no finer calling in life than being a Chicago fireman. Yet all was not pleasant for the boy. He came down with bronchial pneumonia and nearly died. A neighbor brought over a set of lead soldiers for Dutch to play with, and they became his favorite toys.

Jack Reagan was a drinker, which didn't help the family's finances. Ronald Reagan later remembered that his mother "had to make a soup bone last several days and be creative in her cooking." Fried liver was considered a Sunday feast.

The boys did their part too. In the summer, Nelle would hang a sack of fresh-popped popcorn around each of their necks and send them out to peddle it in front of White City amusement park, a mile away on 63rd Street—child labor laws were loose then. That same summer, the lake cruiser *Eastland* capsized in the Chicago River. Jack Reagan took his older son downtown to watch the recovery efforts. Dutch stayed home with Mom.

Sometime in 1916, the Reagan family left Chicago and moved to Galesburg. It's not clear whether Jack quit his Loop job or was fired. Their time in Hyde Park was over.

Many years later, President Reagan told a friend that he had once lived in Chicago but didn't know the address. The Reagans were not listed in any

Ronald Reagan's childhood Chicago home, 832 East 57th Street. *Photo by the author.*

of the contemporary city directories or telephone books. Reagan had always been frank about his father's drinking, so now the friend thought to look in old arrest records. He finally found a listing for Jack Reagan of 832 East 57th Street, charged as a "drunk and disorderly."

Now that the Reagan family's Chicago home had been located, in 1986 the Commission on Chicago Landmarks declared the 832 East 57th Street building to be "noteworthy due to historical associations." However, it was denied landmark status. The commission felt that the future president hadn't lived there long enough.

In 2004 the University of Chicago became owner of the building. As part of the long-range expansion plans for its hospital, the university was buying up the surrounding properties. For several years afterward, tenants continued to rent the flats, while the occasional Reagan fan showed up on pilgrimage. Then, in 2012, the university announced that the building would be torn down.

A few newspapers lamented the impending destruction. A few preservationists launched a protest. Perhaps if Chicago didn't have its own sitting president—or perhaps if Reagan had been a Democrat—the 57th Street building would have been saved. In 2013 the Chicago home of America's fortieth president was demolished. Today, the site is a parking lot.

EDGEWATER BEACH HOTEL

A grand hotel will contribute to the mystique of a city. Chicago still has some great ones. And the city has lost some great ones too. We remember their names fondly—Sherman, Morrison, LaSalle and Great Northern are a few of them.

If any lost Chicago hotel could be called legendary, it was the Edgewater Beach. The name said it all. The hotel was located at 5349 North Sheridan Road, in the heart of the Edgewater neighborhood, with its own private beach.

The hotel was born through an unusual set of circumstances. In 1915 John T. Connery and John Corbett owned several parcels of land along Sheridan Road north of Foster Avenue. When Connery's attempt to buy the Chicago Cubs failed, he began looking for another investment opportunity. Meanwhile, architect Benjamin Marshall was planning to put up an apartment building just north of Connery and Corbett's holdings. Connery, Corbett, Marshall and Charles E. Fox (Marshall's business partner) wound up pooling their resources to incorporate the Edgewater Beach Hotel Company.

Marshall designed a four-hundred-room, Spanish-style stucco building for the site. Arranged in the form of a Maltese cross, so that most of the rooms would have a view of the lake, the Edgewater Beach Hotel opened on June 3, 1916. It was an immediate success. In 1924 a six-hundred-room annex was added. An apartment building, the Edgewater Beach Apartments, opened north of the main hotel in 1928.

Of course, the 1,200-foot-long private beach was one of the hotel's main selling points. That beach had been the source of controversy. Even before the hotel was built, when the site was still sand dune, Connery and Corbett tried to establish how far into the lake their property extended. They were challenged in court by other local property owners, who argued that the partners' plans were cutting off public access to the lake. The challenge ultimately failed.

The hotel continued to develop other attractions to go with its beach. The complex eventually included a tennis court, pitch-and-putt golf course, gardens and a children's playground. A private bus shuttled guests to Marshall Field's Loop store. For a while, the hotel even had a seaplane to fly people downtown. The Edgewater Beach was a full-service resort.

There was entertainment too. Glenn Miller, Tommy Dorsey, Xavier Cugat and other stars of the big band era played the Edgewater Beach. The

Edgewater Beach Hotel postcard. *Author's collection.*

music was broadcast live over the hotel's own radio station, WEBH. The ballroom did a big business in weddings, proms and college dances.

One notorious incident spoiled the fun. Because the Edgewater Beach was only two miles from Wrigley Field, it was a convenient place to stay for visiting baseball teams. In 1949 Philadelphia Phillies first baseman Eddie Waitkus was shot in the hotel by a deranged female fan. The event became the basis for the novel (and movie) *The Natural*.

Waitkus eventually recovered from his wounds, and the shooting didn't have any lasting effect on business. But in 1954 the city extended Lake Shore Drive to Hollywood Avenue on landfill, cutting off the hotel from the lake. And as air conditioning became more common, the Edgewater Beach lost another of its advantages.

By now the hotel had been sold to an investors syndicate. The new management tried to adapt to the changing times. To make up for the loss of the private beach, an outdoor swimming pool and cabana were built. One of the dining rooms was redone in a Polynesian theme. A playhouse operated for a few years, featuring such talent as Groucho Marx and Rita Moreno.

In 1962 the hotel was again sold. Attempting to rebrand the Edgewater Beach as an affordable venue, the latest owner cut costs. Maintenance was deferred, occupancy dropped and entire wings of the hotel were closed. As the downward spiral continued, the once-elegant pink palace began to look shabby.

On December 12, 1967, the Edgewater Beach filed for bankruptcy. A few days later, the hotel closed. Loyola University converted the building into a dorm, but that didn't last. In 1970 the hotel was demolished. Today, all that remains of the complex is the Edgewater Beach Apartments, at Sheridan and Bryn Mawr.

THE ORIGINAL OLD ST. MARY'S

Chicago is justly proud of its historic churches. When one of them is threatened with demolition, there is usually a public outcry, and many venerable buildings have been saved. One that was not saved was Old St. Mary's Church—the original Old St. Mary's.

St. Mary of the Assumption was the city's first Catholic church, built in 1833 on Lake Street just west of State. Six years later, the entire balloon-frame building was moved a few blocks away to Michigan Avenue at Madison. In 1843 a brick replacement church was erected on the southwest corner of Madison and Wabash. When Chicago was established as a diocese later that year, it became the city's Catholic cathedral.

The Great Fire of 1871 destroyed St. Mary's Cathedral. Afterward, Bishop Thomas Foley decided to rebuild his cathedral north of the river, in Holy Name Parish. Meanwhile, he needed a temporary cathedral. In 1872 Foley purchased the Plymouth Congregational Church.

Located outside the fire's path, on the southeast corner of Wabash Avenue and 9th Street, Plymouth Congregational had been built in 1865. The architect was Gourdon P. Randall. A few months after the fire, the church had been the site of a mass meeting at which the Chicago Public Library was founded. On October 9, 1872, it was re-consecrated as St. Mary's Catholic Church.

The Wabash Avenue St. Mary's served as a cathedral for three years. Although the Lemont limestone building had its charms, it was not considered grand enough to be the seat of the bishop of a growing diocese. The *Chicago Times* described St. Mary's Pro-Cathedral as "a dumpish building without a spire, and entirely destitute in accommodations for the sanctuary, high altar, and sacristy." With the dedication of Holy Name Cathedral in 1875, St. Mary's reverted to its status as an ordinary church.

In 1903 the parish was placed under the direction of the Paulist Fathers order of priests. The decades passed. The South Loop went into a long decline. Anyone with money moved out. By the 1930s, the area had become mostly commercial—and what wasn't commercial was slum. Aging gracefully while the neighborhood deteriorated, the church remained one rock of stability. People began calling it Old St. Mary's.

As early as 1904, the Paulists had organized a male choir. However, the Paulist Choristers really came into their own after Father Eugene O'Malley took over in 1928. At its peak, the choir had sixty-five singers and was internationally famous. When Bing Crosby played a "singing priest" in the movie *Going My Way*, his character was named—not coincidentally—Father O'Malley.

The church was distinctive in other ways. "Old St. Mary's runs along without the Holy Name society, the Altar & Rosary society, and the young people's sodalities that help the pastor in most parishes," a 1955 article reported. "It has no parishioners except a few permanent residents of the big Michigan Avenue hotels. Yet Old St. Mary's is filled every Sunday." The pews were filled even at 3:00 a.m, for its night-owl Mass. In those days, Catholics were expected to attend weekly Mass on Sunday itself and not on anticipated Saturday evening.

Despite its historic pedigree, Old St. Mary's fell victim to progress. In 1970 the property was sold to the Standard Oil Company of Indiana. The official explanation was that the building had become too expensive to repair and would be razed in 1975.

That was in June. In mid-September, it was announced that the schedule had been revised. Old St. Mary's would close at the end of the month and then be demolished. Gossip said that the archdiocese wanted to act before preservationists had a chance to organize.

The final Mass was held on September 27, 1970. Father O'Malley was asked to be part of the closing ceremonies but declined. "I don't want to," he told his friends. "I wish they could have saved the church." Shortly afterward, Old St. Mary's was leveled, replaced by a parking lot.

From 1971 until 2002, the parish operated out of a new building at Wabash and Van Buren. Today, the latest Old St. Mary's is located at 1500 South Michigan Avenue. And on the southeast corner of Wabash and 9th, the parking lot remains.

Peter Hand Brewery

Today, Chicago has a number of microbreweries to quench the discerning thirst. Our subject here is the city's last macrobrewery.

Peter Hand was a Prussian-born brewer. After serving in the Union army during the Civil War, he came to Chicago and went to work at the Conrad Seipp Brewing Company. In 1891 Hand opened a small brewery of his own at North and Sheffield Avenues, in the heart of the city's German community. He called his beer Meister Bräu ("Master Brew").

Hand died in 1899, but his brewery survived, one of dozens serving the Chicago market. In 1920 it was officially closed because of Prohibition. When the dry law was repealed in 1933, Peter Hand Brewing Company resumed operation. Business was good, and the plant was expanded several times.

Most of the small neighborhood breweries had died with Prohibition. A few came back to reestablish themselves as Meister Bräu's local competitors. On the North Side, the Atlantic Brewing Company produced Tavern Pale Dry. Peter Fox Brewing Company brewed Fox DeLuxe Beer on the West Side, as did Monarch Brewing Company with Monarch Beer. Atlas Brewing turned out Atlas Prager and Edelweiss on the South Side. Also on the South Side was the Manhattan Brewing Company, home of Canadian Ace. That was the mob's brewery.

Then, during the 1950s, the beer industry began changing. Large breweries swallowed their smaller rivals. One by one, local brands were bought up or driven out of business by growing national brands like Budweiser, Schlitz and Pabst.

In 1965 a group of investors purchased the Peter Hand Brewery. Convinced that small breweries were doomed, they decided to expand to a national market. The company was renamed Meister Bräu Incorporated and went public, with an initial stock offering of 1.2 million shares common and 500,000 shares preferred. Two more production sites were added, with the purchase of breweries in Toledo and San Francisco.

Now Meister Bräu began an aggressive marketing campaign. The company sponsored White Sox, Blackhawks and Bulls broadcasts. Bottle openers, beer steins, coasters and posters were given away. The number of Meister Bräu billboards around the city was exceeded only by those reading "Daley for Mayor."

The brewery also sponsored a popular radio program, *The All-Night Meister Bräu Showcase*. Hosted by veteran broadcaster Franklyn MacCormack, the show ran six nights a week, from 11:05 p.m. through 5:30 a.m., on WGN. MacCormack blended light music with poetry readings and stories, for the ultimate in easy listening. The late hour and the power of WGN's "super-

The last of its kind in Chicago—Peter Hand Brewery, 1000 West North Avenue. *Photo by the author.*

station" meant that the broadcasts were heard through much of the country, including places were Meister Bräu was not yet sold. The brewery boasted that MacCormack fans from other states often took home a six-pack or two of Meister Bräu as a souvenir of a Chicago visit.

Meanwhile, the company became a pioneer in low-calorie beer. Meister Bräu Lite was introduced in 1967, using a formula first developed for an unsuccessful brew called Gablinger's Diet Beer. Lite sales took off. Soon the brewery added a line of other products under the Lite banner, including party dips and dry roasted peanuts.

At first, the expansion seemed to be working. Brewery production rose to more than 1 million barrels per year. But management had overextended. The company started losing money. Then, in 1971, Franklyn MacCormack suffered a heart attack during a broadcast and died shortly afterward. It was an ominous sign.

In June 1972, the Meister Bräu brands—including the popular Lite label—were sold to Miller Brewing of Milwaukee. Two weeks later, the North Avenue brewery filed a petition for bankruptcy. In the spring of 1973, the plant was sold at auction to a partnership led by an experienced Wisconsin brewer.

The new management resurrected an old name, Peter Hand Brewing Company. Its flagship brew was Old Chicago Beer, further playing into the local connection. Although Old Chicago Dark won a few blind taste tests, the brands never caught on. Nor could the company compete with the advertising dollars of the big national breweries. In 1978 the Peter Hand Brewery closed for a final time. The property at North and Sheffield is now a strip mall.

THE HOUSES THAT JIMMY BUILT

If you are the president of the United States, you have to decide what to do with the rest of your life once you leave office. Our earliest presidents simply went back home and continued on where they'd left off. Today, there are more options. An ex-president can use his celebrity to write memoirs, give speeches, do consulting or engage in some other activity that will provide a comfortable living.

Jimmy Carter followed his own path. Abraham Lincoln had split wood to build houses before he was president. In 1986, five years after leaving office, Carter came to Chicago to build houses.

Along with his wife, Rosalyn, Carter was working as a volunteer at Habitat for Humanity, a Georgia-based Christian ministry that constructed homes for the poor. The couple had first become involved with Habitat two years earlier. Then they'd helped renovate a six-story apartment in New York City. In Chicago they would be building a new four-unit townhouse in the West Garfield Park neighborhood, on the southeast corner of Maypole and Kildare Avenues.

The Carters arrived at O'Hare Airport in the early hours of Sunday, July 6. They'd just completed a seventeen-hour flight from Zimbabwe, where the former president had taken part in an Independence Day celebration. Rosalyn went off to their son's apartment in Evanston to catch up on their laundry. Jimmy came into the city to check out the building site and examine the blueprints.

During their week in Chicago, the Carters decided to live near the townhouse project. "We prefer to stay with the people with whom we are working," the ex-president told reporters. On Monday they moved into a one-bedroom apartment on the seventh floor of the Guyon Hotel, at Washington and Pulaski. By 1986 the big old building had seen better days. News reports described the Guyon's frayed carpets, bare light bulbs, crumbling plaster and spray-painted gang graffiti.

But once a POTUS, always a POTUS. Although no special cleanup was done before Carter's arrival, the hotel's elevators were inspected and

Homes built by former president Jimmy Carter at 4255 West Maypole Avenue. *Photo by the author.*

the smoke detectors checked. The Secret Service also settled in. Agents followed Carter everywhere, and at least one man was always on guard outside his apartment.

The other Guyon residents were happy to have Carter living among them. "We were shocked; we just didn't believe he would be up here," one woman said. "It shows that he cares."

More than a hundred people worked on the townhouse. Among them were seventy volunteers from local building trades unions. Future residents were also on the job, giving them "sweat equity" in their home. The sixty-one-year-old ex-president himself often clocked fourteen-hour days. One afternoon he took time off from sawing and hammering to dedicate the site of a future Habitat project in Uptown.

Rainy weather hampered construction that week. Still, the first unit was completed in four days. On Friday afternoon, the new family moved in. The mother had worked alongside the others all week long and was happy to be leaving a rat-infested tenement a few blocks away. "I love you all," she told Carter and the rest. "If it weren't for you, I wouldn't be here."

Jimmy Carter's Chicago week closed that evening with a Habitat reception at the Fourth Presbyterian Church on Michigan Avenue. Mayor Harold Washington praised Carter for the example he was setting for others. The mayor hoped that the former president would continue his good work and would return often to Chicago. Habitat founder Millard Fuller also thanked Carter for all he was doing to publicize the ministry's mission.

Three decades later, Habitat for Humanity still builds housing for people in poverty. The ex-president's participation eventually evolved into an annual Carter Work Project. Thirty years after its Chicago week, the "building blitz" was reported to have constructed affordable housing for more than 3,800 families in fourteen countries. More than 90,000 volunteers from all parts of the world had participated.

Unfortunately, the West Garfield Park townhomes that Carter helped build eventually became derelict. They were torn down in 2010. The Guyon Hotel still stands at 4000 West Washington Boulevard. It has been abandoned, and its future is uncertain.

The Wandering Monument

Each generation writes its own history of the past. Sometimes new facts are discovered that challenge established perceptions. Sometimes current sensitivities are used to judge earlier persons or events. Even things "written in stone" are subject to change.

In the summer of 1812, the United States and Britain went to war. Many native tribes saw the war as a chance to get rid of the Americans who'd moved into their lands, an idea the British encouraged. Fort Dearborn was an American outpost at the mouth of the Chicago River. With the local Potawatomis growing hostile, the fort's commander, Captain Nathan Heald, received orders to evacuate his garrison and the civilian population.

On the morning of August 15, Heald's party of ninety-three people left the fort and began moving south along the lakeshore. The captain thought he'd reached an agreement for safe passage with the Potawatomis. But before his party had gone very far, the Potawatomis ambushed them. More than fifty of the evacuees were killed and the rest taken prisoner. Most of the captives were later ransomed, although some died in captivity. The event became known as the Fort Dearborn Massacre. Considered an important milestone in Chicago history, it was later memorialized with the first star on the city's official flag.

Tradition said that the fighting had taken place on the lakefront about two miles south of the fort. In 1893 railroad sleeping car builder George Pullman was living among his fellow tycoons near that site, at 1729 South Prairie Avenue. The city was about to celebrate the World's Columbian Exposition. Pullman decided to erect a monument to the historic 1812 event on his property.

The finished bronze sculpture was the work of Danish sculptor Carl Rohl-Smith. Set on a stage-like base, it measured eight by nine feet and was five feet deep. A famous incident in the battle is portrayed—the Potawatomi chief Black Partridge is raising a hand to rescue Margaret Helm from another tomahawk-wielding Potawatomi. Rohl-Smith gave his work the title *The Fort Dearborn Massacre.*

The monument remained in place until 1931. By then Pullman was dead, the millionaires had abandoned Prairie Avenue and the neighborhood had become a run-down industrial district. The monument itself was neglected and vandalized.

Pullman's will had left the monument to the Chicago Historical Society, in trust for the people of Chicago. Now the monument was refurbished and moved to the lobby of the society's headquarters on Clark Street. There it stayed for decades. Schoolteachers often used it as an instructional tool on class field trips.

Vintage postcard picturing Chicago's wandering monument. *Author's collection.*

Massacre is a loaded word. The original version of the story was that the Potawatomis had double-crossed Captain Heald after guaranteeing a safe conduct. However, later historians noted that Heald had promised to leave behind supplies and whiskey at the abandoned fort but had not kept that promise. The Potawatomis had attacked because they felt Heald had double-crossed them. Reflecting this alternative narrative, in 1972 the monument was given the subtitle "The Potawatomi Rescue."

Still, some native groups felt that the monument was racist. There were protests against it. During the 1980s, when Prairie Avenue was being restored as a historic district, the historical society turned its hot potato over to the City of Chicago. Rohl-Smith's sculpture was moved back to its old neighborhood and displayed on the grounds of the Clarke mansion.

That lasted until 1997. The city was preparing to re-dedicate the property around the Clarke mansion as the Hillary Rodham Clinton Women's Park. Female empowerment was to be celebrated. Margaret Helm, the woman in the monument, was obviously a victim. So Rohl-Smith's sculpture was removed from the grounds and placed in storage in a city warehouse.

In 2009 the Battle of Fort Dearborn Park was dedicated at 1801 South Calumet Avenue. Recent scholarship has determined that the battle actually took place a bit farther north, near what is now Roosevelt Road. However, the city decided to stay with the traditional site.

When the new park was being planned, it seemed that the wandering monument might find a permanent home there. That proposal was opposed by native groups, and nothing was done. Presumably, after more than twenty years, Carl Rohl-Smith's most controversial work is still sitting in that warehouse.

HENRY W. RINCKER HOUSE

For decades into the 1970s, the Lilac Farm grocery store stood near the southwest corner of Milwaukee and Devon Avenues. Customers rarely gave a thought to the old frame house behind the store. Neighborhood kids knew it only as "the haunted house."

Then, in 1978, a developer bought the 5.2 acres of land that included Lilac Farm, the house and a few other buildings. He planned on replacing everything with a strip mall and some condos. Now the old house attracted more attention. Research by the city's Commission on Historical and Architectural Landmarks revealed that the house had been built by Henry W. Rincker as long ago as 1851.

Rincker had been born in Germany as Heinrich Wilhelm Rincker in 1818. He came from a family of bell-makers. Arriving in Chicago with his wife in 1846, Rincker established a brass foundry on Randolph Street just east of the river and Americanized his given names. The couple boarded a block from the foundry on Washington Street.

Mrs. Rincker died of cholera in 1849. Henry healed by throwing himself into his work. His foundry prospered. He cast the bells for the new St. Peter's Church and for the Chicago City Hall. In 1851 he remarried. Disease had killed his first wife. For his new bride, Henry Rincker built a new house in the farm country a dozen miles northwest of his foundry. The Milwaukee Plank Road ran right past his front door, making travel into the city convenient.

The Rinckers lived in their home along the plank road only a few years. In 1858 their young daughter died. Haunted by memories, they sold the house and closed the foundry. The Rinckers moved to Fort Wayne, where Henry studied for the ministry. He eventually became a Lutheran pastor in Strasburg, Illinois.

The Rincker House passed through several owners before being purchased by the developer. In October 1978, the landmarks commission issued its report. The report noted that the house had been constructed in an unusual manner—it was actually a brick structure covered with exterior wood siding, the air space between the brick and the wood serving as an effective means of insulation. Besides being a splendid example of Gothic Revival architecture, the 1851 house was the second-oldest building in the city.

In 1979 the Chicago City Council approved landmark status for the house. The developer opposed the action and sought a demolition permit. A compromise was reached, with the developer agreeing to move the Rincker House to another location on the property.

The house was still standing on its original site in February 1980 when vandals set it on fire. Despite heavy damage, firefighters saved most of the building. But the worst was yet to come. Early on the morning of August 25, 1980, a bulldozer appeared on the property and leveled the Rincker House.

What about the landmark designation? The wrecking company had gotten a permit to knock down a structure at 6384 North Milwaukee Avenue, the lot where the Rincker House stood. But the house's official address was listed as no. 6366. When the demo permit was issued for no. 6384, the city computer had not recognized a building with protected status. What about the large signs on

"Demolished by Mistake"—the landmark Henry W. Rincker House, 6366 North Milwaukee Avenue. *Photo by the author.*

the Rincker House that proclaimed it a city landmark? The bulldozer operator said he hadn't seen them.

An investigation was launched. The city filed a $1 million lawsuit, saying that the demolition "diminished Chicago's cultural and historic stock and destroyed manifestations of Chicago's past accomplishments." One politician upped the ante, filing a $75 million class action suit. Another politician was brought to trial for allegedly trying to fix the case and later acquitted. Meanwhile, little more than a mile from the Rincker site, the Mark Noble farmhouse was confirmed as Chicago's oldest building, dating from 1833. That took some of the sting out of the demolition "mistake."

In the aftermath of the demolition, a local historian suggested that the city rebuild the leveled landmark, as Warsaw had done with its bombed-out Old City after World War II. That never happened. A strip mall now occupies the southwest corner of Milwaukee and Devon. And the Henry W. Rincker House remains notorious as an official Chicago City Landmark that was destroyed.

THE GOLD COAST CAVERNS

John Huck rates a footnote in most Chicago history books. In 1871 his North Side home was the last building destroyed by the Great Fire. Less remembered is Huck's peculiar legacy to State Street.

Huck arrived in Chicago from Germany in 1846. A brewer by trade, the next year he established his own brewery next to his residence on Chicago Avenue at Rush Street. Americans had traditionally drunk English-style ale or porter. Huck's brewery was the first in the city to produce the crisper German-style lager.

Huck prospered. Within a few years, he opened Chicago's first beer garden on the tree-lined property next to the brewery. He became a leader in the local German community and active in politics. In 1855 he helped organize the meetings protesting the city's new saloon-closing laws, protests that erupted into the Lager Beer Riot.

Meanwhile, Huck's operations had outgrown the small property on Chicago Avenue. Late in 1855 he began constructing a sprawling complex of brewing buildings and a malt house along what is now the east side of State Street, just north of Goethe. He also moved into a new home on the lakefront at Fullerton Avenue.

By 1871 the John A. Huck Brewery had become one of the largest breweries in the country. Running underneath the property was a series of underground tunnels. They were sunk at a depth of twenty feet to provide a naturally cool storage area for kegs of Huck's beer. The tunnels were finished in masonry and measured ten feet high by twenty feet wide. The entire labyrinth stretched back and forth and around for a distance of nearly two miles.

Like Huck's home, the brewery was destroyed in the 1871 fire. The property along State Street stood vacant for years. In 1878 Huck laid plans to rebuild, but he died before he could start construction. The Huck family scrapped the brewery project and sold the property. During the 1880s, the area began its transformation into the Gold Coast. Elegant mansions rose on the site of old John Huck's brewery. Below ground, the lager tunnels remained. Inevitably, they were discovered by the neighborhood kids.

Exploring the Huck caverns became a rite of passage for a boy wanting to avoid the awful taunt of "Chicken!" The caverns were unlit and it was a time before flashlights, but the youthful explorers were resourceful. They made candle lanterns out of tin cracker boxes and were all set.

Local parents were dismayed. They warned their sons that the caverns sheltered homeless people, fugitives from the law or other disreputables. There were rats down there too. Cave-ins were a constant danger. The caverns were to be strictly avoided!

Naturally, all these lurid tales had the opposite effect on adventuresome boys. The caverns became an even more popular playground. City officials finally bowed to adult pressure, declared the caverns a safety hazard and sealed them off around 1900.

Then, in 1927, work began on the new Ambassador East Hotel on the northeast corner of State and Goethe. The construction crew digging the foundation broke through into a section of the old lager caverns. At first the crew didn't know what they had found. Those particular caverns were filled in, and the hotel soon rose on the site. Once again, the Huck caverns were forgotten—until 1963.

At that point, a number of vintage brownstones north of the hotel were being torn down to make way for a high-rise. A onetime neighborhood resident wrote a letter to the *Chicago Tribune* about the caverns. Soon other old-timers were sharing their memories of subterranean adventures. One elderly man related that his family had never been able to freeze the backyard for ice skating because the water kept seeping into the ground, and even city officials could offer no solution to the problem. Only later did they discover that the water had been draining into the caverns.

Many years have now passed since anyone reported coming across one of John Huck's old lager caverns. Likely they are all gone, but we can't be sure.

Perhaps some of them remain. Perhaps a visionary promoter will locate them and transform them into a tourist attraction.

Atlanta has Underground Atlanta, and Seattle has Underground Seattle. Underground Chicago, anyone?

ARCHER-35TH RECREATION

Not so long ago, Chicago was the bowling capital of the world, with more than one hundred different tenpin palaces. Now there are only about a dozen left within the city. The most historic of these lost landmarks was Archer-35th Recreation, the home of the Petersen Classic.

Louis Petersen came to Chicago from Detroit in the early 1900s. The bowling industry was just starting to grow, and Petersen became a major driver of its growth. By 1913, when he had just turned thirty, he was operating two successful establishments on the city's South Side. He promoted them by offering free instruction, as well as weekly prizes for patrons who rolled high scores. He also organized the first cooperative alliance of local bowling proprietors.

In 1919 Petersen went west to enter the oil business. That venture failed, and two years later he was back in Chicago and back in bowling. His new Archer-35th Recreation occupied the entire second floor of a commercial building at 2057 West 35th Street. It was a big bowling center for its time, with sixteen alleys.

Most bowling proprietors built their business around leagues, groups of bowlers that would contract to roll a weekly schedule over a season of eight or nine months. To supplement his league play, Petersen came up with a new promotion. He would stage the richest bowling tournament in the world.

The first Petersen Classic was held on October 2, 1921. Thirty-two bowlers rolled eight games each in a single day. When they'd finished, Harry Steers had the highest total and received a check for $1,000. That was big money for a sporting event in 1921—the same year, first prize in the U.S. Open golf tournament was only $500.

His tournament was all that Louis Petersen had hoped for. The Petersen Classic became an annual event on the bowling calendar. Like most tournaments, it was dominated by star bowlers, so the number of entries remained small. Petersen wanted to expand. He finally came up with a novel way to attract more bowlers.

His idea was simple: if the winning scores were low, then more people would bowl, figuring they might get lucky and win a big prize.

Archer-35th Recreation, Chicago's most famous bowling alley. *Photo by the author.*

So Petersen did everything he could to keep the scores down. He set up overweight bowling pins. He fixed each alley with high boards that made precise shooting difficult. He hung large portraits of past winners just past the foul line to create a feeling of claustrophobia. He carried on a running stream of commentary over the loudspeaker. And if any bowler overcame all these distractions and threatened to post a high score, the pinboy would suddenly call time and amble over to the washroom for a lengthy break. Such a delay was guaranteed to throw even the best bowlers off their rhythm.

Petersen's plan worked. Scores plummeted. Now bowlers from around the country began making an annual journey to Archer-35th Recreation.

Part of the appeal was the funky old joint itself. Louis Petersen died in 1958, and the operation was taken over by his son-in-law, Mark Collor. About the only modernizing Collor did was replacing the pinboys with pinsetting machines. Everything else looked unchanged from 1921.

A bowler trudged up a dark, narrow flight of stairs from the street and entered a Capone-era saloon. Pass through a gold-painted metal fire door and now he was in the bowling arena. The room smelled of old cigar smoke and stale beer. Half the light bulbs in the ceiling were burned out, so that the sixteen alleys were bathed in sinister shadows.

This was the Petersen Classic. At its peak in the early 1980s, the tournament ran nine months and drew thirty-six thousand contestants. The top prize was

$55,000. Even if a bowler finished in 100th place, he still got $1,000. All for an entry fee of $65.

Then competitive bowling went into decline. Entries fell off. In 1993 Collor was ready to retire. When the building's roof developed a major leak, he closed down the tournament. Archer-35th Recreation was demolished shortly afterward. In the years since, the new Orange Line 'L' has helped revitalize the neighborhood, and townhouses stand on the old bowling site. Today, a much-smaller version of the Petersen Classic is staged each spring in the suburbs.

WESTERN-BELMONT OVERPASS

In 2017 city crews tore down the Western-Belmont overpass. The two-block-long, two-lane viaduct had carried Western Avenue through traffic over the five-corner intersection with Belmont and Clybourn Avenues. The junction of the three streets was once again a normal, at-grade intersection.

The Western-Belmont overpass was a relic of another era. In the first decades of the twentieth century, automobiles and trucks were clogging city streets more and more. Traffic signals were invented and did help move things along, but only so much. Fly-over intersections seemed to be the way of the future. You saw them in the 1927 movie *Metropolis* and other science fiction films.

The Outer Drive sections of Lake Shore Drive were the most notable early use of the grade-separation idea in Chicago. In a few locations, where a city street crossed over a railroad line on a viaduct, that viaduct was extended to pass over an intersecting street as well. The Roosevelt Road viaduct over State Street and the Central Avenue viaduct over Grand Avenue were two examples.

During the 1950s, the city began building a large-scale expressway system. At the same time, a number of overpasses for busy intersections of surface streets were proposed. Archer-Ashland, Ashland-Pershing, Halsted-47th, Ogden-Cermak and Fullerton-Damen were some of the spots being discussed. On South Damen Avenue, a new viaduct between 37th and 47th Streets would open that street to through traffic over Pershing Road and railroad tracks. And there was Western-Belmont.

Back in 1902 the Riverview amusement park opened at the northwest corner of Western and Belmont. The park drew thousands of patrons each day, most of whom arrived on streetcars—one of the lines was even named Riverview-

Larrabee. But by midcentury auto traffic around the park was getting heavier each year. The obvious solution was the overpass on Western Avenue.

The Western-Belmont overpass opened in 1962. The South Damen viaduct was also completed, as were the overpasses at Archer-Ashland and Ashland-Pershing. The other overpass projects were still in the talking stage when outside events caused attitudes to change.

The Western-Belmont overpass did its job well for five years. Then, in 1967, Riverview closed. The vacated property was slow in being developed, so there was much less traffic around. When a new police station was built at the Western-Belmont corner, the viaduct actually impeded its operations.

Meanwhile, on the South Side, operations were tapering off at the Union Stock Yards. The Archer-Ashland and Ashland-Pershing overpasses had been built to ease congestion there. After the yards closed in 1971, these overpasses were also obsolete.

Few people had complained about aesthetics when the overpasses were being built. Once they were no longer needed, critics discovered they were ugly. They cast shadows over buildings and blighted the neighborhood. Yet demolition costs were high. So for decades the overpasses stayed in place. How long would they last? What would the city do when they finally fell apart?

An answer came in 1992, when the North Ogden viaduct over Goose Island showed signs of deterioration. Rather than fix the viaduct, the city

Western Avenue overpass at the Belmont-Clybourn intersection. *Photo by the author.*

tore it down. So now a death-watch began on the three overpasses. During the next ten years, Archer-Ashland and Ashland-Pershing were demolished when they became too expensive to maintain. The South Damen viaduct was also torn down without replacement, even though that left a mile-long gap in a major arterial street.

Meanwhile, the city also eliminated the overpasses at Roosevelt-State and Central-Grand. The new viaducts over the adjacent railroad tracks were truncated so that the streets would intersect at grade. In 2017 the long-discussed Fullerton-Damen improvement was completed. Instead of carrying Fullerton traffic over the Damen-Elston intersection on a viaduct, Elston Avenue was rerouted to intersect with each of the other streets separately.

On the city's far southeast side, another grade-separation project was also finished in 2017. The complex junction of Torrence Avenue with 130th Street and Brainard Avenue was rebuilt, but as an underpass. Although this type of engineering is more expensive than putting up a viaduct, it is our current way of the future. The Western-Belmont overpass was likely the last of its kind in Chicago.

Part V

DRIVE-BY NEIGHBORHOODS

ALBANY PARK

During the 1920s, scholars at the University of Chicago identified seventy-five distinct "Community Areas" within the city of Chicago. Later studies expanded this number to seventy-seven. Aside from those tweaks, the neighborhood boundaries established ninety years ago have remained constant. City government has given them official recognition, for statistical and planning purposes.

Albany Park is Community Area 14. Roughly speaking, it extends from the Chicago River west to Elston Avenue and from Montrose Avenue north to Foster Avenue.

The first permanent settlers arrived in the area during the 1840s, mostly German and Swedish farmers. William Spikings was among them. He built a brick farmhouse at what is now 4853 North Pulaski Road and lived in it for more than seventy years, watching the city grow out to him.

These early settlements were part of the town of Jefferson. After Chicago annexed Jefferson in 1889, developers moved in. One of them called his subdivision Albany Park, after his native city in New York, and this became the name for the greater community.

Although streetcars ran on Lawrence Avenue as early as 1896, the real growth of Albany Park dates from the coming of the 'L'—then known as the Ravenswood branch—in 1907. Soon the blocks surrounding the Kimball-

Lawrence terminal were filled with massive apartments. Only the lakefront had a denser concentration of buildings. Lawrence Avenue became the major business street. Commercial strips also developed along Montrose and Kedzie.

Away from the terminal, the apartments thinned out. East of Kedzie, in the streets near a bend in the river, a charming enclave of brick bungalows developed. Known as Ravenswood Manor, it featured the highest-priced housing stock in the greater community area. The section west of Crawford Avenue (Pulaski Road) also became a bungalow belt. This neighborhood was part of an older settlement known as Mayfair.

Raw numbers tell the story. The 1910 census counted about seven thousand people living in Albany Park. Ten years later the figure had grown to twenty-seven thousand. Another ten years and the population was over fifty-five thousand.

Haugan School was expanded several times until it stretched over an entire city block, becoming Chicago's largest elementary school. Roosevelt High School grew so crowded that the nearby Von Steuben School was converted into another high school. The city widened Kimball Avenue, and in 1931 the street got its own bus line.

Most of the people moving to Albany Park in these years were eastern European Jews. They came from West Town, North Lawndale and the

Albany Park—apartment phalanx on Central Park Avenue. *Photo by the author.*

Maxwell Street area. They built temples, schools, community centers, theaters and all manner of businesses. Albany Park became the center of Jewish life in Chicago.

Community Area 14 remained stable through the 1950s. But the city was evolving, movement to the suburbs accelerating. More people were driving cars. And if you didn't need a bus or the 'L', why bother to live in a congested area of apartment hulks?

By 1970 Albany Park was in trouble. Much of the Jewish population had dispersed. Crime rose, property values fell and storefronts became vacant. The neighborhood was on its way to becoming a slum when new vigor arrived with a new wave of immigrants.

The latest arrivals were from many places—the Middle East, the Balkans, East Asia, different Spanish-speaking countries. The population decline was halted. Albany Park became one of the city's most ethnically diverse communities. Now more than forty different languages were heard in the local public schools. Koreans were especially visible. On the storefronts along the shopping strips, Asian characters replaced the Hebrew letters. A portion of Lawrence Avenue was given the honorary designation of Seoul Drive, with the adjacent area nicknamed Korea Town.

More recently, the Hispanic population has been growing the fastest. Of the fifty-two thousand Albany Park residents counted in the 2010 census, about half were Hispanic. Non-Hispanic whites numbered 29 percent, and Asians were 14 percent. African Americans were counted at 4 percent.

Through more than a century of change, Albany Park has endured. You can't really call it a typical Chicago community—a "representative" community might be a better way to put it. Some of it is pretty, some of it is gritty. But Albany Park is never boring.

CICERO

Cicero is not part of the city of Chicago. Cicero is a suburb, about seven miles west-southwest of the Loop. Yet in physical appearance, it looks enough like the city that you might think it was just another one of those Community Areas instead of a separate political entity.

Cicero Township was established in the 1860s, with an original size of thirty-six square miles. Over the next few decades, Chicago nibbled away at its outer sections, while Oak Park and Berwyn went their own ways. In 1901 the remaining six square miles of the original township were incorporated as the town of Cicero. The borders of the town—12th Street to 39th Street, the Belt Line railroad to 62nd Avenue—have remained in place since then.

Cicero did not grow outward from a single point. Rather, a number of separate settlements gradually came together and coalesced. These included communities like Clyde, Drexel, Hawthorne and Morton Park. The new town had excellent railroad transportation and low taxes, and industry was attracted to Cicero. By the 1920s Cicero had become the second-largest manufacturing center in all Illinois. The population grew from sixteen thousand in 1900 to more than sixty thousand in 1930. By that time the town boasted 115 factories.

The largest manufacturer was the Hawthorne Works, at Cicero Avenue and 22nd Street (Cermak Road). Opened in 1905, the plant made telephones and related equipment for the Western Electric Company. The factory complex eventually spread over 141 acres, with more than a hundred buildings covering 2.5 million square feet of floor space. At its peak, more than forty thousand people worked at Hawthorne.

During the 1920s Cicero also became home to another growing industry: organized crime. Prohibition was the law of the land. With Chicago mayor William E. Dever cracking down on bootlegging, Al Capone moved his operations to Cicero. He established headquarters at the Hawthorne Hotel, just down the block from Hawthorne Works.

Soon Capone was running the town. In one famous incident, he slapped Cicero's mayor down the steps of the city hall, while the local cops watched and did nothing. Frequent gun battles erupted, and it was said that "if you smell gunpowder, you know you're in Cicero." Capone returned to Chicago in 1927, but Cicero's reputation was firmly established.

Still, the town wasn't all factories and gangsters. During the early years of aviation, the Cicero Flying Field was among the country's largest aerodromes. Two race courses, Sportsman's and Hawthorne, drew big crowds. Cicero was also home to Morton Junior College, one of the first community colleges, known to locals as UCLA—University of Cicero Located on Austin.

People put down roots in Cicero. The population held steady at around sixty-five thousand for decades. Most of the residents were Czechs who had moved west from Pilsen and South Lawndale. There were also a large number of Poles. The Cermak Road strip became known for several restaurants featuring eastern European dishes.

One group that wasn't found in Cicero was African Americans. In 1951 a black family who tried to move into an apartment on 19th Street was met

Cicero—a 1920s shift change at Hawthorne Works. *Author's collection.*

with violence. Three nights of rioting ensued, the National Guard was called in and the family was forced to leave.

Cicero's factories weathered tough times during the Depression. World War II and the 1950s brought some rebound. Then there was a long, slow decline as jobs moved away. In 1983 Hawthorne Works closed. Today, a strip mall occupies the property. All that's left of the historic complex is its signature tower.

Although some factories still remain, Cicero has also tried to adapt to a post-industrial environment. New life was brought in with the entrance of a large Latino population. The 2010 census revealed Cicero had about eighty-three thousand residents, with more than three-fourths of those identifying as Hispanic. Many of the old restaurants along Cermak have given way to establishments serving Mexican food.

Today, Morton College occupies a modern building on Central Avenue and maintains a museum dedicated to the Hawthorne Works. Cicero is the home of the Chicagoland Sports Hall of Fame. There is still racing at Hawthorne Race Course. Each fall mushroom lovers celebrate the annual Houby Festival. Cicero survives and moves onward.

ENGLEWOOD

Englewood is a mini-Detroit. Well into the second half of the twentieth century, the area centered on 63rd and Halsted Streets was dynamic and prosperous. In more recent times, the community has struggled to overcome a host of urban problems.

The history of Englewood begins in the 1850s with the coming of the railroads. Two lines crossed near what is now 63rd and Wentworth. A settlement called Junction Grove took root nearby. Some years later, a local real estate developer popularized the name Englewood, after his home town of Englewood, New Jersey.

Most of the early settlers here were German and Irish. Railroad workers lived near the junction, and truck farmers occupied the land to the west. When the Stock Yards opened a few miles up Halsted, many of the people employed there also found homes in Englewood.

In 1865 Englewood became part of the town of Lake. The Cook County Normal School and the first Englewood High School were built during the decades that followed. The entire area was annexed by Chicago in 1889. Soon after the annexation, plans were announced for a world's fair, to be held in nearby Jackson Park.

The 1893 Columbian Exposition set off a minor building boom in Englewood. Among the builders was Dr. Henry H. Holmes, who constructed a hotel on the southwest corner of 63rd and Wallace. Later it was discovered that the supposed doctor had used the hotel to rob and murder as many as two hundred people, making him America's first serial killer. Today, the Englewood Post Office occupies the site of the Holmes "Murder Castle."

As Englewood moved into the new century, the community continued to grow. Brick two-flats and apartment buildings joined the older wooden cottages. Banks, schools, hospitals, churches and other institutions of modern civilization were established. The city streetcar system was extended into the area, and in 1907, Englewood got its own 'L' branch. The population passed ninety thousand and kept going.

The focus of the community was 63rd and Halsted. With three major department stores and hundreds of smaller businesses, this became the busiest shopping district outside the Loop. More than that, it was the busiest outlying shopping district in the United States. For decades the stores here rang up more sales than many medium-size cities.

Englewood came through the Depression and World War II in reasonably good shape. The real challenges developed in the years after 1950. Now

Englewood—new construction along 63rd Street. *Photo by the author.*

more people were driving cars and moving to the suburbs. Shopping malls like Evergreen Plaza began drawing traffic away from 63rd and Halsted. The marginal stores closed, and many of the better ones left.

Meanwhile, expressway construction and urban renewal in other parts of the city displaced many African Americans. Some of these families settled in Englewood. Panic-peddling and white flight followed. In 1950 blacks were 11 percent of the local population. That number increased to 69 percent in 1960 and 96 percent ten years later.

During the 1970s, the city made a concerted effort to revive the 63rd-Halsted shopping center. Traffic was diverted away from the intersection, and the two key streets became bus-only malls. The experiment failed. The last two anchor stores, Sears and Wieboldt's, eventually pulled out.

Englewood continued going downhill. The crime rate became one of the highest in the nation. Homes were abandoned or torched, leaving whole blocks empty. By 2010 the population had dwindled to just thirty thousand. Englewood was looking a lot like…well, a lot like Detroit.

If a single building symbolized Englewood during these years, it was the South Side Masonic Temple, at 6400 South Green Street. Opened with much fanfare in 1921, the massive seven-story brick structure served the order until 1965, when it was repurposed as a community center. After that, several other attempts at adapted reuse followed and failed. The temple was finally abandoned in the early 2000s and stood vacant until it was demolished in 2018.

Yet Englewood has not given up. Much of the southern section remains stable. Here and there, some new houses have been built. At 63rd-Halsted, the relocated Kennedy-King College and new stores have helped restore focus to the community's historic heart. And once again like Detroit, Englewood hopes to be the new urban frontier.

HEGEWISCH

This is the most remote corner of Chicago. You are twenty-two miles from State and Madison. You can drop a coin and have it roll into Indiana, yet you are still within the corporate limits of Chi-Town. You must be in Hegewisch.

The name of the neighborhood is pronounced "*heg*-wish," and it takes in all of Chicago east of Lake Calumet and south of 118th Street. According to the boundaries drawn up by University of Chicago social scientists and officially adopted by the city, this is Community Area 55.

Most of the land here is marshy. In the 1850s, railroads from the east began to push through on their way to Chicago. Adolph Hegewisch was involved in the industry as president of the United States Rolling Stock Company, a builder of railroad cars. He wanted to establish his own "ideal workingman's community," like George Pullman was doing on the other side of Lake Calumet. And like George Pullman, Hegewisch would name the new town after himself.

In 1883 Mr. H bought 100 acres of land near the rail yards, at what is now Brandon and 135th, and opened his factory. The presence of the factory attracted speculators, who purchased an additional 1,500 acres to the north. A few streets were laid out, and some houses were built. There was talk of digging a canal through Wolf Lake to Lake Michigan to lure industry to the community.

Adolph Hegewisch had predicted that his Hegewisch would attract ten thousand people. Soon it became clear that it was just too far away from everything. In 1889 the City of Chicago annexed the area anyway. And as the decades went by, other entrepreneurs came with their own grand plans. Those didn't work out either.

The population of Hegewisch edged up to seven thousand during the 1920s. Most of the people were of eastern European stock, with Poles the largest group. Nearly half of the population was foreign born. Many of them worked in the steel mills, in the nearby Ford assembly plant or in the old rail yards off Brainard Avenue.

Hegewisch—crossing the border into Indiana on 134th Street. *Photo by the author.*

The community had a collection of small stores along Brandon and Baltimore Avenues. The nearest large shopping district was in the South Chicago neighborhood, around 92nd and Commercial. There were also some stores across the border in Indiana.

Downtown Chicago seemed light years away. Few local people had cars. The South Shore railroad was fast but expensive. If you wanted to get to the Loop, there was a single-track streetcar line that crossed the swamp to the north. With a few transfers, you might make it downtown in under two hours.

Hegewisch stayed stuck through the Depression and World War II. With peace after 1945, the long-awaited boom finally exploded. New yellow brick ranch houses sprang up on the boggy prairie, and the population finally passed Adolph Hegewisch's ten-thousand-person benchmark. Off 134th Street near the Indiana border, there was even a trailer park. Now the neighborhood was drawing police, firefighters and municipal workers who were required to live within the city limits.

In 1976 Hegewisch earned a somber footnote in Chicago history. On the morning of December 20, Mayor Richard J. Daley came out to dedicate the new field house at Mann Park, sinking a half-court basket in the process. It was the longtime mayor's last public appearance. That afternoon he died of a heart attack.

Fifteen years later, Hegewisch itself nearly died. Now the mayor was Richard M. Daley, and he floated a proposal to replace all of Community

Area 55 with a new airport. In the end, federal officials vetoed the plan because of safety concerns.

Hegewisch was hit hard by the departure of the steel industry. The 2010 census recorded a population of 9,426. Although that number represents a continuing decline, Hegewisch doesn't look like a community in decline. The homes are neat and tidy. The old business strips along Brandon and Baltimore have been spruced up. Wolf Lake continues to draw recreational traffic.

But one thing you won't find in Hegewisch is a gas station. With Indiana just a short drive away, most locals fill up over the border and save some cash. What could be smarter?

MOUNT GREENWOOD

Mount Greenwood is the far southwest corner of Chicago. This is Community Area 74, about fourteen miles from the Loop. Compared to the rest of the city, it looks fairly new. But Mount Greenwood has a long history.

During the last half of the nineteenth century, Chicago was the fastest-growing city in the world. That fact meant there would one day be a great need for a certain type of real estate—namely, cemeteries. In 1879 George Waite plotted a cemetery in a farming area near 111th Street and Sacramento Avenue. Because it sat on a ridge with an abundance of trees, Waite named his cemetery Mount Greenwood.

Within a few years, other cemeteries opened for business near Waite's burying ground. This was the era before automobiles, so horse-drawn funerals were all-day affairs. A collection of restaurants and saloons developed along 111th Street, to refresh mourners before they made the long journey back to the city.

The 111th Street strip also attracted a less dignified clientele. Two racetracks—one for horses, one for dogs—were located a few miles to the west, as were a number of brothels. So despite all the dead residents, Mount Greenwood was getting a rowdy reputation. The Village of Morgan Park wanted to annex the area and shut down the saloons. Fearing such a fate, in 1907 local property owners chartered their own village.

Mount Greenwood was an independent municipality for twenty years. The big event of that time was the Battle of the Ditch. Mount Greenwood Cemetery had a drainage ditch. The village passed an ordinance against the ditch, saying it polluted their drinking water. When the cemetery ignored the law, the villagers took up picks and shovels and filled in the ditch themselves.

The year was 1916, and for the locals this conflict loomed larger than the ongoing war in Europe.

In 1927 Mount Greenwood had about three thousand residents. Yet there were no streetlights, no sewers, few paved streets and drinking water drawn from wells. The citizens voted to become part of Chicago—just in time for the Great Depression.

Years passed. The Depression dragged on. More people moved into Mount Greenwood, but the public improvements lagged behind. During the late 1930s, federal money became available to implement those long-overdue projects—just in time for World War II.

The war ended in 1945. The public works construction was finally pushed through, and Mount Greenwood grew. The national flight to the suburbs was on, although in this case, the suburb was part of the city. Mount Greenwood's population hit twelve thousand in 1950 and ten years later passed the twenty thousand mark.

Most of the postwar settlers were Irish Catholic. Today, when many religious high schools have closed, Mount Greenwood still supports three of them, and St. Xavier University is also part of the community. The main cluster of these institutions, along Central Park Avenue, forms a regular Catholic Campus. Local son John R. Powers wrote a whimsical account of his youth in *The Last Catholic in America* and its two sequels. As a salute to the cemeteries, Powers called the neighborhood the Seven Holy Tombs.

Mount Greenwood—postwar homes along Central Park Avenue. *Photo by the author.*

By 1984 nearly all the old truck farms had been subdivided. The last Mount Greenwood farm, on land southeast of 111th Street and Pulaski Road, was also the last remaining farm within the Chicago city limits. The Board of Education purchased the property. Today, it is the site of the Chicago High School for Agricultural Science.

Mount Greenwood has become a mature, fully built community. Yet it doesn't feel crowded. Most of the homes are single family, and the business establishments are small; there are parks and open space within the Catholic Campus and along the railroad. Having the farm and all those cemeteries helps too.

Then we have this:

> FIRST MAN (running up frantically): Where can I find a cop?
> SECOND MAN: Try Mount Greenwood.

That comedy club routine always got a laugh. And it's true—Community Area 74 is home to many police officers and others who are required to live within the city. The 2010 census counted a Mount Greenwood population of 19,093, broken down as 86 percent white, 7 percent Hispanic and 5 percent African American.

PORTAGE PARK

First you have to know what the word *portage* means. Think of it as soggy land between two waterways. In our case, we are talking about the area between the Chicago River and the Des Plaines River.

Go back a few hundred years. A Potawatomi would paddle his canoe up one river, get out and carry it five or so miles across the portage and then plunk the canoe down in the other river and start paddling again. If he was lucky, the portage was flooded. Then he could ride that canoe straight through between the two rivers.

Irving Park Road follows the general line of a local portage. So when a park was planned for Irving Park and Central in 1912, it was called Portage Park. That is also the name of the neighborhood around it, Community Area 15.

Settlement actually began in 1841, when an inn was built along the old trail that later became Milwaukee Avenue. Chester Dickinson bought the building a few years later, renamed it Dickinson's Tavern and made it into a popular watering hole. In 1850 local residents organized a town called Jefferson. Naturally, they elected their favorite bartender the first supervisor.

Many legends grew up about Dickinson's Tavern. Abraham Lincoln was supposed to have stayed there, and Stephen Douglas too. One story says that when federal surveyors were plotting Milwaukee Avenue, they arranged a bend in the road so that their buddy Chester would have his tavern prominently displayed. The alternate version is that the surveyors got so drunk they put in the bend by mistake.

During the 1860s the Chicago & North Western railroad laid out a line through the eastern part of the community. The Milwaukee Road followed, and settlements developed near the train stations. The latter railroad also built an east–west spur track to connect with the Cook County poor farm and asylum at Dunning.

The town of Jefferson became part of the city of Chicago in the great annexation of 1889. A few years later electric streetcars came clanging in. People followed. The park was opened and more people came. Developers started building bungalows—hundreds of them.

Ribbon commercial strips developed along the streetcar routes. The major concentration of stores was at the triple intersection of Milwaukee, Irving Park and Cicero. Known as Six Corners, it became one of the city's leading shopping districts. Another major retail center grew up around Belmont and Central, on the community's southern edge.

Portage Park—bungalows along Mason Avenue. *Photo by the author.*

Meanwhile, Dickinson's Tavern fell victim to progress. In 1929 it was recognized as Chicago's oldest brick building, but that didn't save it from the wrecking ball. The historic inn was torn down and replaced by a commercial block, which later gave way to a strip mall.

By 1930 the boundaries of the city's Community Areas were officially established. Portage Park was considered "residentially mature." The population was about sixty thousand, described as middle class and skilled blue-collar. Those characteristics have held up ever since.

What happens when a community reaches residential maturity? It tries to hold its own. That's what Portage Park has been doing for ninety years. Drive down most of the side streets and the bungalows and two-flats look much the same as they did in the 1920s.

The business districts have not done as well. When people bought cars and abandoned public transit, there was less need for ribbon commercial strips. Six Corners and Belmont-Central remained prosperous into the 1990s. Today, along Milwaukee or Irving Park or Belmont, there are many vacant storefronts.

The 2010 census revealed that the population of Portage Park is sixty-four thousand. About 54 percent are identified as white, with Poles the largest ethnic group. Hispanics number 39 percent, with Asians and African Americans accounting for the rest.

Portage Park has many local points of interest. The Portage Theatre still stands near the site of Dickinson's Tavern. Cinema fans make pilgrimages to Chris's Billiards, where scenes from *The Color of Money* were filmed. Architecture tours often include the Karl Stecher House and the Peoples Gas building. At St. John's Lutheran Church, you can find Chicago's last "church bowling alleys." In the center of it all is the park itself, with its tree-lined walks and Olympic swimming pool. And, of course, there are the bungalows.

ROGERS PARK

Rogers Park is located on Chicago's far northeast corner. Based on that geographical fact, this is officially designated as Community Area 1. In general terms, it takes in all of the city north of Devon Avenue and east of Ridge Boulevard.

The earliest residents here were the Potawatomis, who established villages along the glacial ridge that is now Ridge Boulevard. The land eastward toward the lake was too swampy for much of anything. When white

Americans moved in, they stuck to the high ground. In 1839 Philip Rogers built a cabin on the ridge and began truck farming. Over the next several years, other farmers settled in Mr. Rogers's neighborhood.

Patrick Touhy, the founder's son-in-law, really spurred development. During the 1860s Touhy organized many of the locals into a building and land association. The Chicago & North Western extended a line through the area, and in 1878, the village of Rogers Park was incorporated.

Growth was slow but steady. Large Victorian homes were erected in the blocks between the C&NW line and the ridge. A small commercial district sprang up just east of the train station, around Clark and Lunt. In 1885 a second commuter line was completed through the eastern lowlands by the Chicago, Milwaukee & St. Paul Railroad.

Rogers Park was a sleepy little community of 3,500 people when Chicago annexed it in 1893. But as the century turned, 'L' service came to Rogers Park over the CM&SP right-of-way. And then Rogers Park began to awaken. Loyola University relocated from the West Side to a campus at Devon and Sheridan. Two-flats and large apartment blocks went up near the 'L', and the Howard line became the city's busiest. The population jumped from 6,700 in 1910 to more than 57,000 twenty years later.

Rogers Park did not have a single dominant shopping district. Most stores were small and locally owned and could be found in clusters near the 'L' stations. Clark Street had the main streetcar line and developed its own commercial ribbon. Howard Street was a special case. The street bordered Evanston—which was dry—so a whole range of bars and liquor stores set up on the Chicago side of Howard. "Going to Howard" was a favorite field trip for generations of Northwestern University students.

East of the 'L', the border with Evanston jumped north of Howard to include the few blocks up to Calvary Cemetery. Here the narrow streets were crammed with three-story apartment buildings that shaded the sidewalks the entire day. Someone called the area the Jungle, and the name stuck.

In Patrick Touhy's day, most people in Rogers Park were English in ancestry. They were later joined by Germans and some Irish. Beginning in about 1910, a significant number of Russian Jews began moving into the community. By 1950, when the population peaked at sixty-three thousand, they were the largest identifiable ethnic or religious group.

Rogers Park was a good place to live. Public transit was fast, stores were plentiful, crime was low, rents were affordable and Lake Michigan was at your doorstep. That last fact was important in the era before air conditioning. The temperatures near the lake could be as much as twenty degrees cooler

Rogers Park—neighborhood beach near the Evanston border. *Photo by the author.*

than a few miles inland. On hot summer weekends the beaches would be filled, and residents might expect to welcome long-lost relatives and friends.

During the 1970s, like many Chicago communities, Rogers Park began to have problems. Some of the older housing deteriorated. Businesses left. Crime increased. Parts of the Jungle became blighted.

More recently, Rogers Park has shown signs of rebounding. The positive factors still remain. Crime has dropped significantly. New construction has replaced many run-down buildings. The Gateway Centre Plaza has helped stabilize the area around the 'L' terminal.

Go up to that 'L' platform at Howard Street. You will see a sign with red-yellow-purple horizontal bars, indicating the three lines that stop there. It looks like a country's national flag, and this is an appropriate metaphor for today's Rogers Park. According to the most recent figures, Rogers Park is one of the city's more diverse communities, its fifty-five thousand residents identifying as 43 percent white, 27 percent African American, 21 percent Hispanic and 6 percent Asian.

WEST GARFIELD PARK

West Garfield Park is Chicago Community Area 26. As the name indicates, it is the first neighborhood you come upon after passing through Garfield Park itself, about five miles due west of the Loop.

Settlement here actually predates the park. A plank road was laid along the line of Lake Street in the early 1840s, closely followed by Chicago's first railroad in 1848. The railroad became the Chicago & North Western and later built train shops near today's Keeler Avenue.

In 1869 the West Side Park Board created three major parks. The middle one, straddling Madison Street, was called Central Park. A small settlement developed just to the west, also calling itself Central Park. But when President James Garfield was assassinated in 1881, the park became Garfield Park, and the fledging settlement became West Garfield Park. Today, the only reminder of those original names is Central Park Avenue.

During the 1880s the newly renamed community really got going. New construction sprang up in the blocks near the park. There were single-family homes and some large apartments, although two-flats were predominant. Graystone was especially popular.

A gentlemen's trotting club operated along the east side of Crawford Avenue (now Pulaski Road) south of Madison Street. The Garfield Park Race Track became a center of controversy after gambling kingpin Mike McDonald took over in 1888. There were shootings and one near riot, and neighbors feared for their property values. The track closed for good in 1906.

In 1893 the West Side's first elevated railroad—another Mike McDonald project—went up over Lake Street. This line was soon joined by the Garfield Park Branch of the Metropolitan 'L' at Harrison Street. Now downtown Chicago was only minutes away. More people flocked to West Garfield Park.

The community reached residential maturity in 1919. The largest ethnic group was the Irish, and the St. Mel's complex on Washington Boulevard took on impressive proportions. There was also a significant Russian Jewish settlement. The shopping district along Madison Street was one of the busiest outside the Loop. With four thousand seats, the Marbro was among the city's largest theaters. The nearby Paradise was slightly smaller but was often called "the world's most beautiful movie house."

Cultural institutions included an active West Side Historical Society and the Legler Regional Branch of the Chicago Public Library. Paradise owner J. Louis Guyon opened a new hotel—the Guyon—down the block from his theater. The Midwest Athletic Club was completed in 1928, the tallest building between the Loop and Des Moines, Iowa.

Then came the Great Depression, followed by World War II. West Garfield Park stagnated but remained stable. During the 1950s, African Americans began moving into the community. They were usually met with hostility. Panic-peddling by real estate companies scared longtime residents into selling. Others

West Garfield Park—commercial hub at Madison and Pulaski. *Photo by the author.*

were forced out by construction of the Congress (Eisenhower) Expressway. West Garfield Park changed from all-white to all-black within ten years.

Many homes and businesses were destroyed in a 1965 riot. The trouble developed after a fire truck leaving the Wilcox Street firehouse knocked over a light pole, killing a woman. More of West Garfield Park burned down following the murder of Martin Luther King Jr. in 1968. The big movie theaters closed and major retailers left. Crime rose.

Some people held on, while others left. Vacant lots became common. In 1961 the Chicago Transit Authority had added a new Kostner Avenue station to its Congress (Blue Line) 'L' route, to take care of the heavy business. Less than twenty years later, the number of passengers had dropped so much that the station was shuttered.

The 2010 census recorded a population of eighteen thousand, down from more than fifty thousand in the community's glory days. Yet positive signs remain. There are still stores around Madison-Pulaski, and they still draw customers. Some residential blocks have been rehabbed. The Tilton School is an architectural gem designed by Dwight Perkins. The nearby Garfield Park Conservatory is again drawing people to the area.

A century ago, West Garfield Park promoted itself as being "only five miles from the Loop." That location is still a selling point. What the future will bring to the community remains to be seen.

ABOUT THE AUTHOR

John R. Schmidt is a fifth-generation Chicagoan. He earned his PhD in history at the University of Chicago and has taught at all levels, from kindergarten through college, including more than thirty years in the Chicago Public School System. He has published nearly four hundred articles in magazines, newspapers, encyclopedias and anthologies. This is his fifth book.

Visit us at
www.historypress.com

Printed in the USA
CPSIA information can be obtained
at www.ICGtesting.com
LVHW061334260824
789299LV00004B/144

9 781540 239662